p94 Thai Broiled Chicken

p124 Satay w. Peanut Sauce (chicken)

p84 Thin pancakes

TASTE
OF THE
EAST

TASTE
OF THE
EAST

With over 200 recipes and 1000 photographs
Deh-Ta Hsiung • *Rafi Fernandez* • *Steven Wheeler*

Photography by Edward Allwright

SMITHMARK

This edition published in 1994
by SMITHMARK Publishers Inc.
16 East 32nd Street
New York
NY 10016
USA

SMITHMARK books are available for bulk purchase for sales promotion and premium
use. For details write or call the manager of special sales,
SMITHMARK Publishers Inc.
16 East 32nd Street
New York
New York 10016

Reprinted in 1995

Editorial Director: Joanna Lorenz
Project Editor: Lindsay Porter
Copy Editor: Laura Washburn
Designer: David Rowley
Photography: Edward Allwright
Styling: Maria Kelly

Printed and bound in Singapore

Typeset by MC Typeset Ltd

CONTENTS

TASTE OF CHINA

DEH-TA HSIUNG

China is a vast country – about the same size as Western Europe or the United States – and its climate and food products are similarly varied. Consequently, each region has a very distinctive style of cooking, resulting in the world's most diverse cuisine.

Yet the fundamental character of Chinese cooking remains the same throughout the land. From Peking in the north to Canton in the south and Shanghai in the east to Sichuan in the west, different ingredients are all prepared, cooked and served in accordance with the same centuries-old principles.

THE PRINCIPLES OF CHINESE COOKING

Chinese cooking is distinguished from all other food cultures in its emphasis on the harmonious blending of color, aroma, flavor and texture both in a single dish and in a course of dishes for a meal.

Balance and contrast are the key words, based on the ancient Taoist philosophy of yin and yang. Consciously or unconsciously, any Chinese cook, from the housewife to the professional chef, will work to this yin-yang principle, and will vary ingredients, shapes, seasonings and cooking methods accordingly.

In order to achieve this, two important factors should be observed: the degree of heat and duration of cooking, which in turn means applying the right cooking method to the right food. The size and shape of a particular ingredient must be appropriate to the chosen method of cooking. Ingredients for quick stir-frying, for instance, should be cut into small, thin slices or shreds of uniform size, instead of large, thick chunks. This is not just for the sake of appearance, but because ingredients of the same size and shape will retain their natural color, aroma, and flavor and achieve the required texture if they are cooked for the same amount of time.

EQUIPMENT AND UTENSILS

There are only a few basic implements essential to Chinese cooking and equivalent equipment is always available in a Western kitchen. However, authentic Chinese cooking utensils are of an ancient design, are usually made of inexpensive materials, and have been in continuous use for several thousand years. They do serve a special function, which is not always fulfilled by their more sophisticated and expensive Western counterparts.

Chinese cleaver (1) This is an all-purpose cook's knife used for slicing, shredding, peeling, crushing and chopping. Different sizes and weights are available.

Ladle and spatula (2) Some wok sets consist of a pair of stirrers in the form of a ladle and spatula. Of the two, the flat ladle or scooper (as it is sometimes called) is more versatile. It is used by Chinese cooks for adding ingredients and seasonings to the wok as well as for stirring.

Sand-pot (casserole) (3) Made of earthenware, casseroles are always used for braising and slow cooking on the stove top as they retain an even heat.

Steamer (4) The traditional Chinese steamer is made of bamboo, and the modern version is made of aluminium. The wok can also be used as a steamer with a rack or trivet and the dome-shaped wok lid.

Strainer (5) There are two basic types of strainer. One is made of copper or steel wire with a long bamboo handle, the other of perforated iron or stainless steel. Several different sizes are available.

Wok (6) The round-bottomed iron wok conducts and retains heat evenly. Because of its shape, the ingredients always return to the centre where the heat is most intense. The wok has many functions. It is ideal for deep-frying because its shape requires far less oil than the flat-bottomed deep-fryer. It also has more depth, which means more heat is generated, and a larger cooking surface, which means more food can be cooked at one time. Besides being a frying pan, the wok is also used for braising, steaming, boiling and poaching – in fact, the whole spectrum of Chinese cooking methods can be executed in one single utensil.

INGREDIENTS

Agar-agar (1) Also known as isinglass (*Kanten* in Japanese), agar-agar is a product of seaweed and is sold dried in paper-thin strands or powdered form. Gelatin may be substituted.

Baby corn cobs (2) Baby corn cobs have a wonderfully sweet fragrance and flavor, and an irresistible texture. They are available both fresh and canned.

Bamboo shoots (3) Bamboo shoots are available in cans only. Once opened, the contents may be kept in fresh water in a covered jar for up to a week in the refrigerator. Try to get winter bamboo shoots, which have a firmer texture. Ready sliced bamboo shoots are also available.

Tofu (4) This custard-like preparation of puréed and pressed soya beans is exceptionally high in protein. It is usually sold in cakes about 3in square and 1in thick and can be found in Oriental and health food stores. It will keep for a few days if submerged in water in a container and placed in the refrigerator.

Bean sprouts (5) Fresh bean sprouts, from mung or soya beans, are widely available from Oriental stores and all supermarkets. They can be kept in the refrigerator for two to three days.

Black bean sauce (6) Black bean sauce is made up of salted black beans crushed and mixed with flour and spices (such as ginger, garlic or chili) to make a thickish paste. Sold in jars or cans; once opened, it should be kept in the refrigerator.

Chili bean sauce (7) Chili bean sauce is made from fermented bean paste mixed with hot chili and other seasonings. Sold in jars, some chili bean sauces are quite mild, but some are very hot. You will have to try out the various brands yourself to see which one is to your taste.

Chili oil (8) Chili oil is made from dried red chilies, garlic, onions, salt and vegetable oil. It is used more as a dip than as a cooking ingredient.

Chili sauce (9) This is a very hot sauce made from chilies, vinegar, sugar and salt. Usually sold in bottles, it should be used sparingly in cooking or as

a dip. Tabasco sauce can be a substitute.

Cilantro (11) Fresh cilantro leaves, also known as Chinese parsley are widely used in Chinese cooking as a garnish.

Dried Chinese mushrooms (shiitake) (12) These highly fragrant dried mushrooms are sold in plastic bags. They are not cheap, but a small amount will go a long way, and they will keep indefinitely in an airtight jar. Soak them in warm water for 20–30 minutes (or in cold water for several hours), squeeze dry, and discard the hard stalks before use.

Egg noodles (13) There are many varieties of noodles in China – ranging from flat, broad ribbons to long and narrow strands. Both dried and fresh noodles are available.

Five-spice powder (14) A mixture of star anise, fennel seeds, cloves, cinnamon bark and Sichuan pepper make up five-spice powder. It is highly piquant, so should be used very sparingly, and will keep indefinitely in an airtight container.

Ginger root (15) Fresh ginger, sold by weight, should be peeled and sliced and finely chopped or shredded before use. It will keep for weeks in a dry, cool place. Dried ginger powder is no substitute.

Hoi Sin sauce (16) This tasty sauce is also known as barbecue sauce, and is made from soy beans, sugar, flour, vinegar, salt, garlic, chili and sesame seed oil. Sold in cans or jars, it will keep in the refrigerator for months.

Inapa cabbage (10) There are two widely available varieties of Inapa cabbage (also known as Chinese cabbage) found in supermarkets and greengrocers. The most commonly seen variety has a pale green color and tightly-wrapped elongated head, and about two-thirds of the cabbage is stem which has a crunchy texture. The other variety found has a shorter and fatter head with curlier, pale yellow or green leaves, and white stems.

Oyster sauce (17) This soya based, thickish sauce is used as a flavoring in Cantonese cooking. Sold in bottles, it will keep in the refrigerator for months.

Plum sauce (18) Plum sauce has a unique fruity flavor – a sweet and sour sauce with a difference.

Red bean paste (19) This reddish-brown paste is made from puréed red beans and crystallized sugar. Sold in cans, the left-over contents should be transferred to a covered container and will keep in the refrigerator for several months.

Rice vinegar (20) There are two basic types of rice vinegar – red vinegar is made from fermented rice and has a distinctive dark color and depth of flavor; white vinegar is stronger in flavor as it is distilled from rice.

Rice wine (21) Chinese rice wine, made from glutinous rice, is also known as 'Yellow wine' (*Huang Jiu* or *Chiew* in Chinese), because of its golden amber color. The best variety is called Shao Hsing or Shaoxing from the southeast of China. A good dry or medium sherry can be an acceptable substitute.

Rock sugar (22) Rock sugar is made with a combination of cane sugar and honey. It adds a special sheen to foods that have been stewed with it.

Salted black beans (23) Salted black beans are very salty and pungent. They are sold in plastic bags, jars or cans and should be crushed with water or wine before use. The beans will keep almost indefinitely in a covered jar.

Sesame oil (24) Sesame oil is sold in bottles and widely used in China as a garnish rather than for cooking. The refined yellow sesame oil sold in Middle Eastern stores is not so aromatic, has less flavor and therefore is not a very satisfactory substitute.

Sichuan peppercorns (25) Also known as *farchiew*, these are wild red peppers from Sichuan. More aromatic but less hot than either white or black peppers, they do give quite a unique flavor to the food.

Soy sauce (26) Sold in bottles or cans, this most popular Chinese sauce is used both for cooking and at the table. Light soy sauce has more flavor than the sweeter dark soy sauce, which gives the food a rich, reddish color.

Straw mushrooms (*Volvariella volvacea*) (27) Grown on beds of rice straw, hence the name, straw mushrooms have a pleasant slippery texture and a subtle taste. Canned straw mushrooms should be rinsed and drained after opening.

Water chestnuts (28) Water chestnuts are not nuts as they are the roots of a plant (*Heleocharis tuberosa*). They are also known as horse's hooves in China, on account of their appearance before the skin is peeled off and are available

fresh or in cans. Canned water chestnuts retain only part of the texture, and even less of the flavor, of fresh ones. They will keep for about a month in the refrigerator in a covered jar, if the water is changed every two or three days.

Wonton skins (29) Made from wheat flour, egg and water, these wafer-thin wonton wrappers are sold in 3in squares from Oriental stores. They can be frozen, and will keep for up to six months.

Woodears (30) Also known as cloud-ears, these are dried black fungus (*Auricularia polytricha*). Sold in plastic bags in Oriental stores, woodears should be soaked in cold or warm water for 20 minutes, then rinsed in fresh water before use. They have a crunchy texture and a mild but subtle flavor.

Yellow bean sauce (31) Yellow bean sauce is a thick paste made from salted, fermented yellow soya beans, crushed with flour and sugar. It will keep in the refrigerator for months if stored in a screw-top jar.

CRISPY SPRING ROLLS

Zha Chu Kuen

These small and dainty vegetarian spring rolls are ideal served as appetizers, or as cocktail snacks. For a non-vegetarian version, just replace the mushrooms with chicken or pork, and the carrots with shrimp.

MAKES 40 ROLLS

Ingredients
8oz fresh bean sprouts
4oz tender leeks or scallions
4oz carrots
4oz bamboo shoots, sliced
4oz mushrooms
3–4 tbsp vegetable oil
I tsp salt
I tsp light brown sugar
I tbsp light soy sauce

I tbsp Chinese rice wine or dry sherry
20 frozen spring roll skins, defrosted
I tbsp cornstarch paste
flour, for dusting
oil, for deep-frying

Cornstarch paste

To make cornstarch paste, combine 4 parts dry cornstarch with about 5 parts cold water and mix well until smooth.

1 Cut all the vegetables into thin shreds, roughly the same size and shape as the bean sprouts.

2 Heat the oil in a wok and stir-fry the vegetables for about 1 minute. Add the salt, sugar, soy sauce and wine or sherry and continue stirring for 1½–2 minutes. Remove and drain the excess liquid, then leave to cool.

3 To make the spring rolls, cut each spring roll skin in half diagonally, then place about 1 tbsp of the vegetable mixture one-third of the way down on the skin, with the triangle pointing away from you.

4 Lift the lower flap over the filling and gently roll once.

5 Fold in both ends and roll once more, then brush the upper edge with a little cornstarch paste, and roll into a neat package. Dust a tray with flour and place the spring rolls on the tray with the flap-side down.

6 To cook, heat the oil in a wok or deep-fryer until hot, then reduce the heat to low. Deep-fry the spring rolls in batches (about 8–10 at a time) for 2–3 minutes or until golden and crispy, then remove and drain. Serve the spring rolls hot with a dipping sauce such as soy sauce or Spicy Salt and Pepper.

DEEP-FRIED SPARERIBS WITH SPICY SALT AND PEPPER

Zha Pai Ku

Ideally, each sparerib should be chopped into 3–4 bite-sized pieces before or after cooking. If this is not possible, then serve the ribs whole.

SERVES 4–6

Ingredients
10–12 baby back pork spareribs, weighing in total about 1½lb, with excess fat and gristle trimmed
about 2–3 tbsp flour
vegetable oil, for deep-frying

Marinade
1 clove garlic, crushed and finely chopped
1 tbsp light brown sugar
1 tbsp light soy sauce
1 tbsp dark soy sauce
2 tbsp Chinese rice wine or dry sherry
½ tsp chilli sauce
few drops sesame oil

Spicy Salt and Pepper

To make Spicy Salt and Pepper, mix 1 tbsp salt with 2 tsp ground Sichuan peppercorns and 1 tsp five-spice powder. Heat together in a preheated dry pan for about 2 minutes over low heat, stirring constantly. This quantity is sufficient for at least six servings.

1 Chop each rib into 3–4 pieces, then mix with all the marinade ingredients, and marinate for at least 2–3 hours.

2 Coat the ribs with flour and deep-fry in medium-hot oil for 4–5 minutes, stirring to separate. Remove and drain.

3 Heat the oil to high and deep-fry the ribs once more for about 1 minute, or until the colour is an even dark brown. Remove and drain, then serve with Spicy Salt and Pepper.

DEEP-FRIED SQUID WITH SPICY SALT AND PEPPER

Jiao Yan You Yu

This recipe is from the Cantonese school of cuisine, where seafood is one of their specialties.

SERVES 4

Ingredients
1 lb squid
1 tsp Ginger juice (see right)
1 tbsp Chinese rice wine or dry sherry
about 2½ cups boiling water
vegetable oil, for deep-frying
Spicy Salt and Pepper
fresh Cilantro leaves, to garnish

Ginger juice

To make Ginger Juice, mix finely chopped or grated fresh ginger with an equal quantity of cold water and place in a damp piece of cheesecloth. Twist tightly to extract the juice. Alternatively, crush the ginger in a garlic press.

1 Clean the squid by discarding the head and the transparent backbone as well as the ink bag; peel off and discard the thin skin, then wash the squid and dry well. Open up the squid and, using a sharp knife, score the inside of the flesh in a criss-cross pattern.

2 Cut the squid into pieces each about the size of an oblong postage stamp. Marinate in a bowl with the ginger juice and wine or sherry for 25–30 minutes.

3 Blanch the squid in boiling water for a few seconds – each piece will curl up and the criss-cross pattern will open out to resemble ears of corn. Remove and drain. Dry well.

4 Deep-fry the squid in hot oil for 15–20 seconds only, remove quickly and drain. Sprinkle with the Spicy Salt and Pepper and serve garnished with fresh cilantro leaves.

BON-BON CHICKEN WITH SESAME SAUCE

Bon Bon Ji

The chicken meat is tenderized by being beaten with a stick (called a *bon* in Chinese), hence the name for this very popular Sichuan dish.

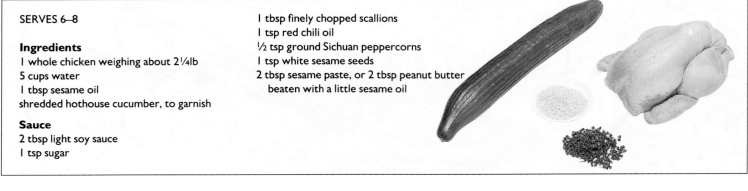

SERVES 6–8

Ingredients
1 whole chicken weighing about 2¼lb
5 cups water
1 tbsp sesame oil
shredded hothouse cucumber, to garnish

Sauce
2 tbsp light soy sauce
1 tsp sugar

1 tbsp finely chopped scallions
1 tsp red chili oil
½ tsp ground Sichuan peppercorns
1 tsp white sesame seeds
2 tbsp sesame paste, or 2 tbsp peanut butter
   beaten with a little sesame oil

1 Clean the chicken well. In a wok or saucepan bring the water to a rolling boil, add the chicken, reduce the heat, and cook, covered, for 40–45 minutes. Remove the chicken and immerse in cold water to cool.

2 After at least 1 hour, remove the chicken and drain; dry well with paper towels and brush on a coating of sesame oil. Carve the meat off the legs, wings and breast and pull the meat off the rest of the bones.

3 On a flat surface, pound the meat with a rolling pin, then tear the meat into shreds with your fingers.

4 Place the meat in a dish with the shredded cucumber around the edge. In a bowl, mix together all the sauce ingredients, keeping a few scallions to garnish. Pour over the chicken and serve.

DEEP-FRIED WONTON SKINS WITH SWEET AND SOUR SAUCE

Cha Won Tun

Ready-made fresh or frozen wonton skins are available from Oriental stores.

SERVES 4–6

Ingredients
16–20 ready-made wonton skins
vegetable oil, for deep-frying

Sauce
1 tbsp vegetable oil
2 tbsp light brown sugar
3 tbsp rice vinegar
1 tbsp light soy sauce
1 tbsp tomato ketchup
3–4 tbsp Basic Stock or water
1 tbsp cornstarch paste

1 Pinch the center of each wonton skin and twist it around to form a floral shape.

2 Deep-fry the floral wonton skins in hot oil for 1–2 minutes, or until crispy. Remove and drain.

3 For the sauce, heat the oil in a wok or saucepan, add the sugar, vinegar, soy sauce, ketchup and stock or water.

4 Thicken the sauce with the cornstarch paste, stirring until smooth, and pour it over the wonton skins. Serve immediately, with extra sauce on the side.

CRISPY 'SEAWEED'

Cai Sung

Surprisingly, this 'seaweed' dish sometimes found in Chinese restaurants is, in fact, ordinary collard greens!

SERVES 4–6	vegetable oil, for deep-frying
	½ tsp salt
Ingredients	I tsp superfine sugar
I lb collard greens	I tbsp ground fried fish, to garnish (optional)

1 Cut off the hard stalks in the center of each collard leaf. Pile the leaves on top of each other, and roll into a tight 'sausage'. Thinly cut the leaves into fine shreds. Spread them out to dry.

2 Heat the oil in a wok or deep-fryer until hot. Deep-fry the shredded greens in batches, stirring to separate them.

3 Remove the greens with a slotted spoon as soon as they are crispy, but before they turn brown. Drain. Sprinkle the salt and sugar evenly all over the 'seaweed'; mix well, garnish with ground fish, and serve.

SESAME SEED-SHRIMP TOASTS

Hsia Jen Tu Ssu

Use uncooked shrimp for this dish, as pre-cooked ones will separate from the bread during cooking.

SERVES 6–8	salt and pepper, to taste	I tbsp cornstarch paste
	I egg white, lightly beaten	I cup white sesame seeds
Ingredients	I tsp finely chopped scallions	6 large slices white bread
8oz shrimp, peeled	½ tsp finely chopped fresh ginger	vegetable oil, for deep-frying
2 tbsp shortening	I tbsp Chinese rice wine or dry sherry	

1 Chop together the shrimps with the shortening to form a smooth paste. In a bowl, mix with all the other ingredients except the sesame seeds and bread.

2 Spread the sesame seeds evenly on a large plate or tray; spread the shrimp paste thickly on one side of each slice of bread, then press, spread-side down, onto the seeds.

3 Heat the oil in a wok until medium-hot; fry 2–3 slices at a time, spread-side down, for 2–3 minutes. Remove and drain. Cut into 6–8 fingers (without crusts).

PICKLED SWEET AND SOUR CUCUMBER

Tan Chu Huang Gua

The 'pickling' can be done in hours rather than days – but the more time you have, the better the result.

SERVES 6–8	2 tsp superfine sugar
	1 tsp rice vinegar
Ingredients	½ tsp red chili oil (optional)
1 hothouse cucumber, about 12in long	few drops sesame oil
1 tsp salt	

1 Halve the unpeeled cucumber lengthwise. Scrape out the seeds and cut across the cucumber into thick chunks.

2 In a bowl, sprinkle the cucumber chunks with the salt and mix well. Leave for at least 20–30 minutes – longer if possible – then drain the juice thoroughly.

3 Mix the cucumber with the sugar, vinegar and chili oil, if using. Sprinkle with the sesame oil just before serving.

HOT AND SOUR CABBAGE

Suan La Pai Cai

Another popular recipe from Sichuan – this dish can be served hot or cold.

SERVES 6–8	3–4 tbsp vegetable oil	1 tbsp light brown sugar
	10–12 red Sichuan peppercorns	1 tbsp light soy sauce
Ingredients	few whole dried red chilies	2 tbsp rice vinegar
1lb pale green or white cabbage	1 tsp salt	few drops sesame oil

1 Cut the cabbage leaves into small pieces each roughly 1 × ½in.

2 Heat the oil in a preheated wok until smoking. Add the peppercorns and chilies.

3 Add the cabbage to the wok and stir-fry for about 1–2 minutes. Add the salt and sugar, continue stirring for another minute, then add the soy sauce, vinegar, and sesame oil. Blend well and serve.

BUTTERFLY SHRIMP

Feng Wei Xia

For best results, use uncooked jumbo shrimp in their shells. Sold headless, they are about 3–4in long, and you should get 18–20 shrimp per pound.

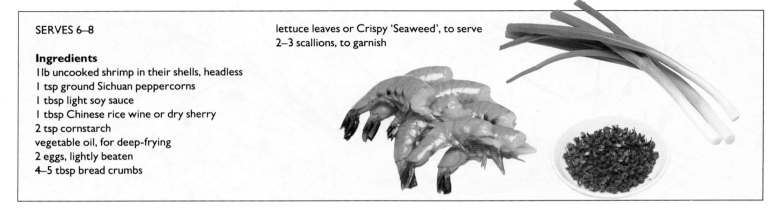

SERVES 6–8

Ingredients
1lb uncooked shrimp in their shells, headless
1 tsp ground Sichuan peppercorns
1 tbsp light soy sauce
1 tbsp Chinese rice wine or dry sherry
2 tsp cornstarch
vegetable oil, for deep-frying
2 eggs, lightly beaten
4–5 tbsp bread crumbs

lettuce leaves or Crispy 'Seaweed', to serve
2–3 scallions, to garnish

1 Peel the shrimp but leave the tails on. Split the shrimp in half from the underbelly, about three-quarters of the way through, leaving the tails still firmly attached.

2 In a bowl, marinate the shrimp with the pepper, soy sauce, wine or sherry, and cornstarch for 10–15 minutes.

3 Heat the oil in a wok or deep-fryer until medium-hot. Pick up one shrimp at a time by the tail, and dip it in the egg.

4 Place the bread crumbs in a shallow dish. Carefully roll the egg-covered shrimp in the bread crumbs.

5 Heat the oil in the wok until medium-hot. Gently lower the coated shrimp into the oil.

6 Deep-fry the shrimp in batches until golden brown. Remove and drain. To serve, arrange the shrimp neatly on a bed of lettuce leaves or Crispy 'Seaweed', and garnish with scallions, which are either raw or have been cooked for about 30 seconds in hot oil.

BASIC STOCK

Qing Tang

The basic stock is used not only as the basis for soup making, but also for general use in cooking whenever liquid is required instead of plain water.

MAKES 10½ CUPS

Ingredients
1½lb chicken pieces
1½lb pork spareribs
15 cups cold water
3–4 pieces fresh ginger, unpeeled and crushed
3–4 scallions, each tied into a knot
3–4 tbsp Chinese rice wine or dry sherry

1 Trim off any excess fat from the chicken and spareribs. With a sharp knife, chop them into large pieces.

2 Place the chicken and spareribs in a large pot or pan with the water. Add the ginger and scallion knots.

3 Bring to a boil and, using a strainer, skim off the froth. Reduce the heat and simmer, uncovered, for 2–3 hours.

4 Strain the stock, discarding the chicken, pork, ginger, and scallions; add the wine or sherry and return to a boil. Simmer for 2–3 minutes. Refrigerate the stock when cool. It will keep for up to 4–5 days. Alternatively, it can be frozen in small containers and defrosted when required.

HOT AND SOUR SOUP

Suan La Tang

This surely must be the all-time favorite soup in Chinese restaurants and take-outs the world over. It is fairly simple to make once you have got all the necessary ingredients together.

SERVES 4

Ingredients
4–6 dried Chinese mushrooms (shiitake), soaked
4oz pork or chicken
I cake tofu
2oz sliced bamboo shoots, drained

2½ cups Basic Stock
I tbsp Chinese rice wine or dry sherry
I tbsp light soy sauce
I tbsp rice vinegar
salt, to taste
½ tsp ground white pepper
I tbsp cornstarch paste

1 Squeeze the soaked mushrooms dry, then discard the hard stalks. Thinly slice the mushrooms, meat, tofu, and bamboo shoots.

2 In a wok or saucepan, bring the stock to a rolling boil and add the sliced ingredients. Bring back to a boil and simmer for about 1 minute.

3 Add the seasonings and bring back to a boil once more. Now add the cornstarch paste and stir until thickened. Serve hot.

CORN AND CRABMEAT/CHICKEN SOUP

Xie Rou Yumi Tang

This soup originated in the USA but it has since been introduced into China. You must use creamed corn in the recipe to achieve the right consistency.

SERVES 4

Ingredients
4oz crabmeat or chicken breast
½ tsp finely chopped fresh ginger
2 egg whites
2 tbsp milk

1 tbsp cornstarch paste
2½ cups Basic Stock
8oz can creamed corn
salt and pepper, to taste
finely chopped scallions, to garnish

1 Flake the crabmeat (or coarsely chop the chicken breast) and mix with the ginger.

2 Beat the egg whites until frothy, add the milk and cornstarch paste and beat again until smooth. Blend with the crabmeat or chicken breast.

3 In a wok or saucepan, bring the stock to a boil, add the creamed sweetcorn, and bring back to a boil once more.

4 Stir in the crabmeat or chicken breast and egg white mixture, adjust the seasonings, and stir gently until well blended. Serve garnished with finely chopped scallions.

CHICKEN AND ASPARAGUS SOUP

Lusun Ji Rou Tang

This is a very delicate and delicious soup. When fresh asparagus is not in season, canned white asparagus is an acceptable substitute.

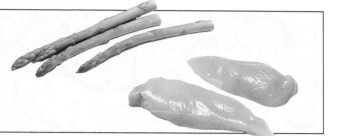

SERVES 4

Ingredients
5oz chicken breast
pinch of salt
1 tsp egg white
1 tsp cornstarch paste

4oz asparagus
3 cups Basic Stock
salt and pepper, to taste
fresh cilantro leaves, to garnish

1 Cut the chicken meat into thin slices each about the size of a postage stamp. Mix with a pinch of salt, then add the egg white, and finally the cornstarch paste.

2 Discard the tough stems of the asparagus, and diagonally cut the tender spears into short lengths.

3 In a wok or saucepan, bring the stock to a rolling boil, add the asparagus, and bring back to the boil, cooking for 2 minutes. (This is not necessary if using canned asparagus.)

4 Add the chicken, stir to separate and bring back to a boil once more. Adjust the seasonings. Serve hot, garnished with fresh cilantro leaves.

SPINACH AND TOFU SOUP

Pao Cai Dao Fu Tang

This soup is delicious. If fresh spinach is not in season, watercress or lettuce can be used instead.

SERVES 4	4oz spinach leaves (weight exclusive of stems)	
	3 cups Basic Stock	
Ingredients	I tbsp light soy sauce	
I cake tofu	salt and pepper, to taste	

1 Cut the tofu into 12 small pieces, each about ¼ in thick. Wash the spinach leaves and cut them into small pieces.

2 In a wok or saucepan, bring the stock to a rolling boil. Add the tofu and soy sauce, bring back to a boil, and simmer for about 2 minutes.

3 Add the spinach and simmer for 1 minute more. Skim the surface to make it clear, then adjust the seasoning and serve.

SLICED FISH AND CILANTRO SOUP

Yu Pian Yen Hsee Tang

It is not necessary to remove the skin from the fish, as it helps to keep the flesh together when cooked.

SERVES 4	2 tsp cornstarch paste	
	3 cups Basic Stock	
Ingredients	I tbsp light soy sauce	
8oz white fish fillet, such as lemon sole or plaice	about 2oz fresh cilantro leaves, chopped	
I tsp egg white	salt and pepper, to taste	

1 Cut the fish into large slices each about the size of a matchbox. Mix with the egg white and cornstarch paste.

2 In a wok or saucepan, bring the stock to a rolling boil and poach the fish slices for about 1 minute.

3 Add the soy sauce and cilantro leaves, adjust the seasonings, and serve.

THREE-DELICACY SOUP

San Xian Tang

This delicious soup combines the three ingredients of chicken, ham and shrimp.

SERVES 4	4oz honey-roast ham
	4oz peeled shrimp
Ingredients	3 cups Basic Stock
4oz chicken breast	salt, to taste

1 Thinly slice the chicken and ham into small pieces. If the shrimp are large, cut each in half lengthwise.

2 In a wok or saucepan, bring the stock to a rolling boil, add the chicken, ham, and shrimp. Bring back to a boil, add the salt, and simmer for 1 minute. Serve hot.

Cook's tip

Fresh, uncooked shrimp impart the best flavor. If these are not available you can use pre-cooked prawns. They must be added at the last stage to prevent over-cooking.

LAMB AND CUCUMBER SOUP

Yang Rou Huang Gua Tang

This is a variation on Hot and Sour Soup, but is much simpler to prepare.

SERVES 4	1 tbsp light soy sauce	3 cups Basic Stock
	2 tsp Chinese rice wine or dry sherry	1 tbsp rice vinegar
Ingredients	½ tsp sesame oil	salt and ground white pepper, to taste
8oz lamb	1 hothouse cucumber piece, about 3in long	

1 Trim off any excess fat from the lamb and discard. Thinly slice the lamb into small pieces. Marinate with the soy sauce, wine or sherry and sesame oil for 25–30 minutes. Discard the marinade.

2 Halve the cucumber piece lengthwise (do not peel), then cut into thin slices diagonally.

3 In a wok or saucepan, bring the stock to a rolling boil, add the lamb, and stir to separate. Return to a boil, then add the cucumber slices, vinegar, and seasonings. Bring to a boil once more, and serve at once.

FRIED SEAFOOD WITH VEGETABLES

Chao San Xian

Another colorful and delicious dish from Southeast China, combining shrimp, squid, and scallops. The squid may be replaced by another fish, or omitted altogether.

SERVES 4

Ingredients
4oz squid, cleaned
4–6 fresh scallops
4oz uncooked shrimp
½ egg white
1 tbsp cornstarch paste
2–3 stalks of celery
1 small red bell pepper, cored and seeded
2 small carrots
about 1¼ cups oil

½ tsp finely chopped fresh ginger
1 scallion, cut into short sections
1 tsp salt
½ tsp light brown sugar
1 tbsp Chinese rice wine or dry sherry
1 tbsp light soy sauce
1 tsp hot bean sauce
2 tbsp Basic Stock
few drops sesame oil

1 Open up the squid and, using a sharp knife, score the inside in a criss-cross pattern. Cut the squid into pieces each about the size of an oblong stamp. Soak the squid in a bowl of boiling water until all the pieces curl up; rinse in cold water and drain.

2 Cut each scallop into 3–4 slices. Peel the shrimp and cut each in half lengthwise. Mix the scallops and shrimp with the egg white and cornstarch paste until well blended.

3 Cut the celery, red bell pepper, and carrots into thin slices, each about the size of a postage stamp.

4 Heat the oil in a preheated wok until medium-hot and stir-fry the seafood for about 30–40 seconds. Remove with a large slotted spoon and drain.

5 Pour off the excess oil, leaving about 2 tbsp in the wok, and add the vegetables with the ginger and scallions. Stir-fry for about 1 minute.

6 Add the seafood to the wok, stir for another 30–40 seconds, then add the salt, sugar, wine or sherry, soy sauce, and hot bean sauce. Blend well, add the stock, and continue stirring for another minute. Then serve garnished with sesame oil.

BRAISED FISH FILLET WITH MUSHROOMS

Chin Chao Yu Tiao

This is the Chinese version of the French *filets de sole bonne femme* (sole with mushrooms and wine sauce).

SERVES 4	2 tbsp cornstarch paste	1 tbsp light soy sauce
	about 2½ cups vegetable oil	2 tbsp Chinese rice wine or dry sherry
Ingredients	1 tbsp finely chopped scallions	1 tbsp brandy
1 lb fillet of lemon sole or plaice	½ tsp finely chopped fresh ginger	about ½ cup Basic Stock
1 tsp salt	4 oz white mushrooms, thinly sliced	few drops sesame oil, to garnish
½ egg white	1 tsp light brown sugar	

1 Trim off the soft bones along the edge of the fish, but leave the skin on. Cut each fillet into bite-sized pieces. Mix the fish with a little salt, the egg white and about half of the cornstarch paste.

2 Heat the oil until medium-hot, add the fish slice by slice and stir gently so the pieces do not stick. Remove after about 1 minute and drain. Pour off the excess oil, leaving about 2 tbsp in the wok.

3 Stir-fry the scallions, ginger, and mushrooms for 1 minute. Add the other ingredients except the cornstarch paste. Bring to a boil. Braise the fish for 1 minute. Thicken with the paste, and garnish.

SHRIMP FU-YUNG

Fu Ron Xia

This is a very colorful dish that is simple to make. Most of the preparation can be done well in advance.

SERVES 4	1 tsp salt	3–4 tbsp vegetable oil
	8 oz uncooked shrimp, peeled	6 oz green peas
Ingredients	2 tsp cornstarch paste	1 tbsp Chinese rice wine or dry sherry
3 eggs, beaten, reserving 1 tsp of egg white	1 tbsp finely chopped scallions	

1 Beat the eggs with a pinch of the salt, and a few bits of the scallions. In a wok, scramble the eggs in a little oil over moderate heat. Remove and reserve.

2 Mix the shrimp with a little salt, 1 tsp of egg white, and the cornstarch paste. Stir-fry the peas in hot oil for 30 seconds. Add the shrimp.

3 Add the scallions. Stir-fry for 1 minute more, then stir the mixture into the scrambled egg with a little salt and the wine or sherry. Blend well and serve.

Sweet and Sour Shrimp

Tang Cu Xia

It is best to use uncooked shrimp if available. If using pre-cooked ones, they can be added to the sauce without the initial deep-frying.

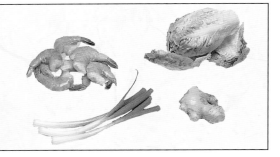

SERVES 4–6	1 tbsp finely chopped scallions
	2 tsp finely chopped fresh ginger
Ingredients	2 tbsp light soy sauce
1 lb jumbo shrimp in their shells	2 tbsp light brown sugar
vegetable oil, for deep-frying	3 tbsp rice vinegar
lettuce leaves, to serve	1 tbsp Chinese rice wine or dry sherry
	about ½ cup Basic Stock
Sauce	1 tbsp cornstarch paste
1 tbsp vegetable oil	few drops sesame oil

1 Carefully pull the soft legs off the shrimp without removing the shells. Dry well with paper towels.

2 Deep-fry the shrimp in hot oil for 35–40 seconds, or until their color changes from gray to bright orange. Remove and drain thoroughly.

3 To make the sauce, heat the oil in a preheated wok, add the scallions and ginger, followed by the seasonings and stock, and bring to a boil.

4 Add the shrimp to the sauce, blend well, then thicken the sauce with the cornstarch paste, stirring until smooth. Sprinkle with the sesame oil. Serve on a bed of lettuce leaves.

STIR-FRIED SHRIMP WITH BROCCOLI

Xi Lan Chao Xia Ren

This is a very colorful dish, highly nutritious and packed with flavor. This recipe can be made with pre-cooked shrimp, in which case you can omit the initial deep-frying.

SERVES 4

Ingredients
6–8oz shrimp, shelled and deveined
1 tsp salt
1 tbsp Chinese rice wine or dry sherry
1 tbsp cornstarch paste
½ egg white
8oz broccoli

about 1¼ cups vegetable oil
1 scallion, cut into short sections
1 tsp light brown sugar
about 2 tbsp Basic Stock or water
1 tsp light soy sauce
few drops sesame oil

1 Cut each shrimp in half lengthwise. Mix with a pinch of salt, and about 1 tsp of the wine, egg white, and cornstarch paste until blended.

2 Cut the broccoli heads into florets; remove the rough skin from the stalks, then slice the florets diagonally into diamond-shaped chunks.

3 Heat the oil in a preheated wok and stir-fry the shrimp for about 30 seconds. Remove with a strainer and drain.

4 Pour off the excess oil, leaving 2 tbsp in the wok. Add the broccoli and scallion, stir-fry for about 2 minutes, then add the remaining salt, and the sugar, followed by the shrimp and stock or water. Add the soy sauce and remaining wine or sherry. Blend well, then finally add the sesame oil and serve.

SQUID WITH GREEN BELL PEPPER AND BLACK BEAN SAUCE

Si Jiao You Yu

This dish is a product of the Cantonese school, and makes an attractive meal that is as delicious as it looks.

SERVES 4

Ingredients
12–14oz squid
1 medium green bell pepper, cored, and seeded
3–4 tbsp vegetable oil
1 clove garlic, finely chopped
½ tsp finely chopped fresh ginger
1 tbsp finely chopped scallions

1 tsp salt
1 tbsp black bean sauce
1 tbsp Chinese rice wine or dry sherry
few drops sesame oil

1 To clean the squid, discard the head, the transparent backbone, and the ink bag. Peel off and discard the skin, then wash the squid and dry well. Open up the squid and, with a sharp knife, score the inside of the flesh in a criss-cross pattern.

2 Cut the squid into pieces each about the size of an oblong postage stamp. Blanch the squid in a pan of boiling water for a few seconds. Remove and drain; dry well.

3 Cut the green bell pepper into small triangular pieces. Heat the oil in a wok and stir-fry the green bell pepper for about 1 minute.

4 Add the garlic, ginger, scallion, salt, and squid, then continue stirring for 1 minute more. Finally add the black bean sauce, and wine or sherry, and blend well. Sprinkle with sesame oil and serve.

FISH WITH SWEET AND SOUR SAUCE

Wu Liu Yu

Another name for this dish is Five-Willow Fish, after the five shredded ingredients in the dressing.

SERVES 4–6

Ingredients
1 carp, bream, sea bass, trout, grouper, or striped
    mullet, weighing about 1½lb, gutted
1 tsp salt
about 2 tbsp all-purpose flour
vegetable oil, for deep-frying
fresh cilantro leaves, to garnish

Sauce
1 tbsp vegetable oil

2oz carrot, thinly shredded
2oz sliced bamboo shoots, drained and shredded
1oz green bell pepper, thinly shredded
1oz red bell pepper, thinly shredded
2–3 scallions, finely shredded
1 tbsp thinly shredded fresh ginger
1 tbsp light soy sauce
2 tbsp light brown sugar
2–3 tbsp rice vinegar
about ½ cup Basic Stock
1 tbsp cornstarch paste

1 Clean and dry the fish well. Using a sharp knife, score both sides of the fish as far in as the bone, making diagonal cuts at intervals of about 1in.

2 Rub the whole fish with salt both inside and out, then coat it from head to tail with flour.

3 Deep-fry the fish in the hot oil for about 3–4 minutes on both sides, or until golden brown. Remove the fish and drain, then place on a heated platter.

4 For the sauce, heat the oil and stir-fry all the vegetables for about 1 minute, then add the seasoning. Blend well, add the stock, and bring to a boil. Add the cornstarch paste, stirring well, until the sauce thickens and is smooth. Pour the sauce over the fish and garnish with fresh cilantro leaves.

Braised Whole Fish in Chili and Garlic Sauce

Gan Shao Yu

This is a classic Sichuan recipe. When served in a restaurant, the fish's head and tail are usually discarded before cooking, and used in other dishes. A whole fish may be used, however, and always looks impressive, especially for formal occasions and dinner parties.

SERVES 4–6

Ingredients

1 carp, bream, sea bass, trout, grouper or
    striped mullet, weighing about 1½lb, gutted
1 tbsp light soy sauce
1 tbsp Chinese rice wine or dry sherry
vegetable oil, for deep-frying

Sauce

2 cloves garlic, finely chopped
2–3 scallions, finely chopped with the white and
    green parts separated

1 tsp finely chopped fresh ginger
2 tbsp hot bean sauce
1 tbsp tomato paste
2 tsp light brown sugar
1 tbsp rice vinegar
about ½ cup Basic Stock
1 tbsp cornstarch paste
few drops sesame oil

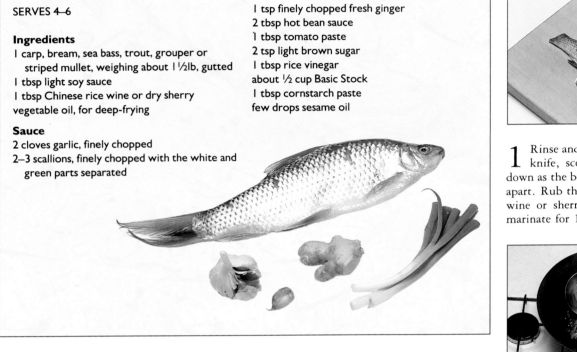

1 Rinse and dry the fish well. Using a sharp knife, score both sides of the fish as far down as the bone with diagonal cuts about 1in apart. Rub the whole fish with soy sauce, and wine or sherry on both sides, then leave to marinate for 10–15 minutes.

2 In a wok, deep-fry the fish in hot oil for about 3–4 minutes on both sides or until golden brown.

3 Pour off the excess oil, leaving about 1 tbsp in the wok. Push the fish to one side of the wok and add the garlic, the white part of the scallions, ginger, hot bean sauce, tomato paste, sugar, vinegar, and stock. Bring to a boil and braise the fish in the sauce for 4–5 minutes, turning it over once. Add the green part of the scallions. Thicken the sauce with the cornstarch paste, sprinkle with the sesame oil, and serve.

STEAMED FISH WITH GINGER AND SCALLIONS

Qing Zheng Yu

Any firm-fleshed fish with a delicate taste, such as salmon or turbot, can be cooked by this same method. The sweet taste of ginger combined with the scallions make this a dish that has long been a firm favorite on mainland China.

SERVES 4–6

Ingredients
1 sea bass, trout or striped mullet, weighing about 1 ½lb, gutted
½ tsp salt
1 tbsp sesame oil

2–3 scallions, cut in half lengthwise
2 tbsp light soy sauce
2 tbsp Chinese rice wine or dry sherry
1 tbsp finely shredded fresh ginger
2 tbsp vegetable oil
finely shredded scallions, to garnish

1 Using a sharp knife, score both sides of the fish as far down as the bone, making several diagonal cuts about 1in apart. Rub the fish all over, inside and out, with salt and sesame oil.

2 Sprinkle the scallions on a heatproof platter and place the fish on top. Blend together the soy sauce, and wine or sherry with the ginger shreds and pour all over the fish.

3 Place the platter in a very hot steamer (or inside a wok on a rack), and steam vigorously, covered, for 12–15 minutes.

4 Heat the oil until hot; remove the platter from the steamer, place the shredded scallions on top of the fish, then pour the hot oil along the whole length of the fish. Serve immediately.

RED AND WHITE SHRIMP WITH GREEN VEGETABLES

Yuan Yang Xia

The Chinese name for this dish is Yuan Yang Shrimp. Pairs of mandarin ducks are also known as *yuan yang*, or love birds, because they are always seen together. They often symbolize affection and happiness.

SERVES 4–6

Ingredients
1 lb uncooked shrimp
pinch of salt
½ egg white
1 tbsp cornstarch paste
6oz snow peas
about 2½ cups vegetable oil
½ tsp salt

1 tsp light brown sugar
1 tbsp finely chopped scallions
1 tsp finely chopped fresh ginger
1 tbsp light soy sauce
1 tbsp Chinese rice wine or dry sherry
1 tsp hot bean sauce
1 tbsp tomato paste

1 Peel and devein the shrimp, and mix with the pinch of salt, the egg white, and the cornstarch paste. Top and tail the snow peas.

2 Heat about 2–3 tbsp of the oil in a preheated wok and stir-fry the snow peas for about 1 minute, then add the salt and sugar and continue stirring for 1 minute more. Remove and place in the center of a warmed serving platter.

3 Heat the remaining oil, partially cook the shrimp for 1 minute, remove, and drain on paper towels.

4 Pour off the excess oil, leaving about 1 tbsp in the wok, and add the scallions and ginger to flavor the oil.

5 Add the shrimp and stir-fry for about 1 minute, then add the soy sauce and wine or sherry. Blend well and place about half of the shrimp at one end of the platter.

6 Add the hot bean sauce and tomato paste to the remaining shrimp in the wok. Blend well and place the 'red' shrimp at the other end of the platter. Serve immediately.

BAKED LOBSTER WITH BLACK BEANS

Jiang Cong Guo Long Xia

The term 'baked', as described on most Chinese restaurant menus, is not strictly correct – 'pot-roasted' or 'pan-baked' is more accurate. Ideally, buy live lobsters and cook them yourself. Pre-cooked ones have usually been boiled for far too long and have lost much of their delicate flavor and texture.

SERVES 4–6

Ingredients
1 large or 2 medium lobsters, weighing about
    1¾lb in total
vegetable oil, for deep-frying
1 clove garlic, finely chopped
1 tsp finely chopped fresh ginger

2–3 scallions, cut into short sections
2 tbsp black bean sauce
2 tbsp Chinese rice wine or dry sherry
½ cup Basic Stock
fresh cilantro leaves, to garnish

1 Starting from the head, cut the lobster in half lengthwise. Discard the legs, remove the claws, and crack them with the back of a cleaver. Discard the feathery lungs and intestine. Cut each half into 4–5 pieces.

2 In a wok, deep-fry the lobster pieces in hot oil for about 2 minutes, or until the shells turn bright orange; remove and drain.

3 Pour off the excess oil leaving about 1 tbsp in the wok. Add the garlic, ginger, scallions, and black bean sauce.

4 Add the lobster pieces to the sauce and blend well. Add the wine or sherry and stock, bring to a boil, and cook, covered, for 2–3 minutes. Serve garnished with cilantro leaves.

BAKED CRAB WITH SCALLIONS AND GINGER

Zha Xie

This recipe is far less complicated to make than it looks. Again, use live crabs if you can to obtain the best flavor and texture.

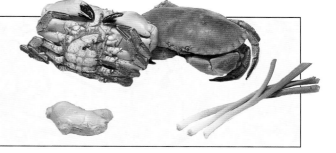

SERVES 4

Ingredients
1 large or 2 medium crabs, weighing about
   1½lb in total
2 tbsp Chinese rice wine or dry sherry
1 egg, lightly beaten
i tbsp cornstarch paste

3–4 tbsp vegetable oil
1 tbsp finely chopped fresh ginger
3–4 scallions, cut into short sections
2 tbsp light soy sauce
1 tsp light brown sugar
about 5 tbsp Basic Stock
few drops sesame oil

1 Cut the crab in half from the underbelly. Break off the claws and crack them with the back of a cleaver. Discard the legs and crack the shell, breaking it into several pieces. Discard the feathery gills and the sac.

2 Marinate with the wine or sherry, egg, and cornstarch paste for 10–15 minutes.

3 Heat the oil in a preheated wok and stir-fry the crab pieces with the ginger and scallions for about 2–3 minutes.

4 Add the soy sauce, sugar, and stock. Blend well and bring to a boil; braise, covered for 3–4 minutes. Sprinkle with sesame oil and serve.

CRISPY AND AROMATIC DUCK

Xiang Cui Ya

Because this dish is often served with pancakes, scallions, hothouse cucumber, and duck sauce (a sweet bean paste), many people mistakenly think this is Peking Duck. This recipe however, uses quite a different cooking method. The result is just as crispy but the delightful aroma makes this dish particularly distinctive. Plum sauce can be substituted for the Duck Sauce.

SERVES 6–8

Ingredients
I oven-ready duckling, weighing about 4½–5lb
2 tsp salt
5–6 whole star anise
I tbsp Sichuan peppercorns
I tsp cloves

2–3 cinnamon sticks
3–4 scallions
3–4 slices fresh ginger, unpeeled
5–6 tbsp Chinese rice wine or dry sherry
vegetable oil, for deep-frying
lettuce leaves, to garnish

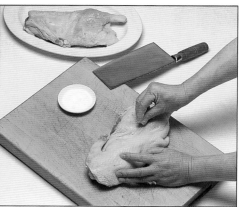

1 Remove the wings from the duck. Split the body in half down the backbone.

2 Rub salt all over the two duck halves taking care to rub it well in.

3 Marinate in a dish with the spices, scallions, ginger, and wine or sherry for at least 4–6 hours.

4 Vigorously steam the duck with the marinade for 3–4 hours (longer if possible), then remove from the cooking liquid and leave to cool for at least 5–6 hours. The duck must be completely cold and dry or the skin will not be crispy.

5 Heat the oil in a wok until smoking, place the duck pieces in the oil, skin-side down, and deep-fry for 5–6 minutes or until crisp and brown, turning just once at the very last moment.

6 Remove, drain, and place on a bed of lettuce leaves. To serve, scrape the meat off the bone and wrap each portion in a pancake with a little sauce, shredded scallion, and cucumber. Eat with your fingers.

Fu-yung Chicken

Fu Ron Ji

Because the egg whites (*Fu-yung* in Chinese) mixed with milk are deep-fried, they have prompted some imaginative cooks to refer to this dish as 'Deep-fried Milk'!

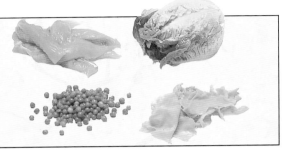

SERVES 4

Ingredients
6oz chicken breast
I tsp salt
4 egg whites, lightly beaten
I tbsp cornstarch paste
2 tbsp milk

vegetable oil, for deep-frying
I lettuce heart, separated into leaves
about ½ cup Basic Stock
I tbsp Chinese rice wine or dry sherry
I tbsp green peas
few drops sesame oil
I tsp finely chopped ham, to garnish

1 Finely grind the chicken meat, then mix with a pinch of the salt, the egg whites, cornstarch paste, and milk. Blend until smooth.

2 Heat the oil in a very hot wok, but before the oil gets too hot, gently spoon the chicken and egg-white mixture into the oil in batches. Do not stir, otherwise it will scatter. Stir the oil from the bottom of the wok so that the *Fu-yung* will rise to the surface. Remove as soon as the color turns bright white. Drain.

3 Pour off the excess oil, leaving about 1 tbsp in the wok. Stir-fry the lettuce leaves with the remaining salt for 1 minute, add the stock, and bring to a boil.

4 Add the chicken to the wok with the wine and peas, and blend well. Sprinkle with the sesame oil and garnish with the ham.

'KUNG PO' CHICKEN – SICHUAN STYLE

Kung Po Ji Ding

Kung Po was the name of a court official in Sichuan; his cook created this dish.

SERVES 4

Ingredients
12oz chicken thigh, boned and skinned
¼ tsp salt
½ egg white, lightly beaten
2 tsp cornstarch paste
1 medium green bell pepper, cored and seeded
4 tbsp vegetable oil

3–4 whole dried red chilies, soaked in water for 10 minutes
1 scallion, cut into short sections
few small pieces of fresh ginger, peeled
1 tbsp sweet bean paste or Hoi Sin sauce
1 tsp hot bean paste
1 tbsp Chinese rice wine or dry sherry
1 cup roasted cashew nuts
few drops sesame oil

1 Cut the chicken meat into small pieces each about the size of a sugar cube. In a bowl, mix together with the salt, egg white, and the cornstarch paste.

2 Cut the green bell pepper into cubes about the same size as the chicken.

3 Heat the oil in a preheated wok. Stir-fry the chicken cubes for about 1 minute, or until the color changes. Remove with a slotted spoon and keep warm.

4 Add the green bell pepper, dried red chilies, scallion, and ginger and stir-fry for about 1 minute; then add the chicken with the bean pastes or sauce and wine or sherry. Blend well and cook 1 minute more. Finally add the cashew nuts and sesame oil. Serve hot.

PEKING DUCK

Bei Jing Ya

This has to be the *pièce de résistance* of any Chinese banquet. It is not too difficult to prepare and cook at home – the secret is to use duckling with a low fat content. Also, make sure that the skin of the duck is absolutely dry before cooking – the drier the skin, the crispier the duck.

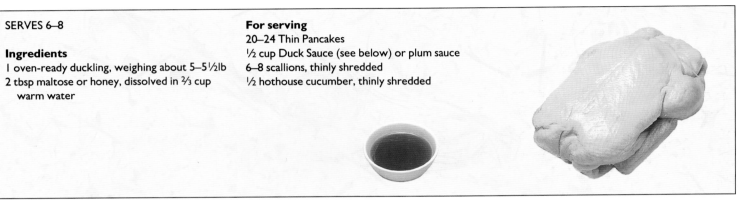

SERVES 6–8

Ingredients
1 oven-ready duckling, weighing about 5–5½lb
2 tbsp maltose or honey, dissolved in ⅔ cup warm water

For serving
20–24 Thin Pancakes
½ cup Duck Sauce (see below) or plum sauce
6–8 scallions, thinly shredded
½ hothouse cucumber, thinly shredded

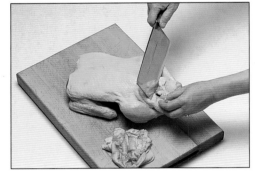

1 Remove any feather studs and any lumps of fat from inside the cavity of the duck. Plunge the duck into a pot of boiling water for 2–3 minutes to seal the pores. This will make the skin airtight, thus preventing the fat from escaping during cooking. Remove and drain well, then dry thoroughly.

2 Brush the duck all over with the dissolved maltose or honey, then hang the duck up to dry in a cool and airy place for 4–5 hours.

3 Place the duck, breast side up, on a rack in a roasting pan, and cook in a preheated oven (400°F) for 1½–1¾ hours without basting or turning.

Duck Sauce

To make Duck Sauce, heat 2 tbsp sesame oil in a small saucepan. Add 6–8 tbsp crushed yellow bean sauce and 2–3 tbsp light brown sugar. Stir until smooth and allow to cool. Serve cold.

4 To serve, peel off the crispy duck skin in small slices using a sharp carving knife or cleaver, then carve the juicy meat in thin strips. Arrange the skin and meat on separate serving plates.

5 Open a pancake on each plate, spread about 1 tsp of sauce in the middle, with a few strips of shredded scallions and cucumber. Top with 2–3 slices of duck skin and 2–3 slices of meat.

6 Roll up the pancake, turn up the bottom edge to prevent the contents from falling out, and eat with your fingers.

SHREDDED CHICKEN WITH CELERY

Qing Cai Chao Ji Si

The tender chicken breast contrasts with the crunchy texture of the celery, and the red chilies add color and flavor.

SERVES 4	½ egg white, lightly beaten	I scallion, thinly shredded
	2 tsp cornstarch paste	few strips fresh ginger, thinly shredded
Ingredients	about 2 cups vegetable oil	I tsp light brown sugar
10oz chicken breast	I celery heart, thinly shredded	I tbsp Chinese rice wine or dry sherry
I tsp salt	I–2 fresh red chilies, seeded and thinly shredded	few drops sesame oil

1 Using a sharp knife, thinly shred the chicken. In a bowl, mix together with a pinch of the salt, the egg white, and the cornstarch paste.

2 Heat the oil in a wok until warm, add the chicken, and stir to separate the shreds. When the chicken turns white, remove with a slotted spoon and drain. Keep warm.

3 In 2 tbsp of oil, stir-fry the celery, chilies, scallion, and ginger for 1 minute. Add the chicken, salt, sugar, and wine. Cook for 1 minute and add the sesame oil. Serve hot.

CHICKEN WITH CHINESE VEGETABLES

Ji Pian Chao Shi Cai

The chicken can be replaced by almost any other meat, such as pork, beef, liver, or shrimp.

SERVES 4	2 tsp cornstarch paste	I scallion, cut into short sections
	4 tbsp vegetable oil	few small pieces fresh ginger, peeled
Ingredients	6–8 small dried Chinese mushrooms (shiitake),	I tsp light brown sugar
8–10oz chicken, boned and skinned	soaked	I tbsp light soy sauce
I tsp salt	4oz sliced bamboo shoots, drained	I tbsp Chinese rice wine or dry sherry
½ egg white, lightly beaten	4oz snow peas, trimmed	few drops sesame oil

1 Cut the chicken into thin slices each about the size of an oblong postage stamp. In a bowl, mix with a pinch of the salt, the egg white, and the cornstarch paste.

2 Heat the oil in a preheated wok, stir-fry the chicken over medium heat for about 30 seconds, then remove with a slotted spoon and keep warm.

3 Stir-fry the vegetables over high heat for about 1 minute. Add the salt, sugar, and chicken. Blend, then add the soy sauce and wine or sherry. Stir a few more times. Sprinkle with the sesame oil and serve.

SOY-BRAISED CHICKEN

Jiang You Ji

This dish can be served hot or cold as part of a buffet-style meal.

SERVES 6–8

Ingredients
1 whole chicken, weighing about 3–3½lb
1 tbsp ground Sichuan peppercorns
2 tbsp finely chopped fresh ginger
3 tbsp light soy sauce
2 tbsp dark soy sauce
3 tbsp Chinese rice wine or dry sherry
1 tbsp light brown sugar
vegetable oil, for deep-frying
about 2½ cups Basic Stock or water
2 tsp salt
1 oz crystallized sugar
lettuce leaves, to garnish

1 Rub the chicken both inside and out with the ground pepper and fresh ginger. Marinate the bird with the soy sauces, wine or sherry, and sugar for at least 3 hours, turning it several times.

2 Heat the oil in a preheated wok, remove the chicken from the marinade and deep-fry for 5–6 minutes, or until brown all over. Remove and drain.

3 Pour off the excess oil, add the marinade with the stock or water, salt, and crystallized sugar and bring to a boil. Braise the chicken in the sauce, covered, for 35–40 minutes, turning once or twice.

4 Remove the chicken from the wok and let it cool down a little before chopping it into approximately 30 bite-sized pieces. Arrange the pieces on a bed of lettuce leaves, then pour some of the sauce over the chicken and serve. The remaining sauce can be stored in the refrigerator to be used again.

CHICKEN AND HAM WITH GREEN VEGETABLES

Jin Hua Yi Shu Ji

The Chinese name for this colorful dish means 'Golden Flower and Jade Tree Chicken'. It makes a marvelous buffet-style dish for all occasions.

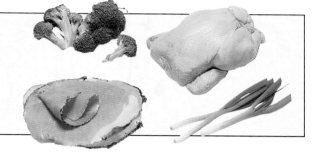

SERVES 6–8

Ingredients
1 whole chicken weighing about 2¼–3lb
2 scallions
2–3 pieces fresh ginger
1 tbsp salt

8oz honey-roast ham
10oz broccoli
3 tbsp vegetable oil
1 tsp light brown sugar
2 tsp cornstarch

1 Place the chicken in a large pan and cover it with cold water. Add the scallions, ginger, and about 2 tsp of the salt. Bring to a boil, then reduce the heat, and simmer for 10–15 minutes under a tightly-fitting cover. Turn off the heat and let the chicken cook itself in the hot water for at least 4–5 hours – you must not lift up the lid, as this will let out the residual heat.

2 Remove the chicken from the pan, reserving the liquid, and carefully cut the meat away from the bones, keeping the skin on. Slice both the chicken and ham into pieces, each the size of a matchbox, and arrange the meats in alternating layers on a plate.

3 Cut the broccoli into small florets and stir-fry in the hot oil with the remaining salt and the sugar for about 2–3 minutes. Arrange the vegetables between the rows of chicken and ham and around the edge of the plate, making a border for the meat.

4 Heat a small amount of the chicken cooking liquid and thicken with the cornstarch. Stir until smooth, then pour it evenly all over the chicken and ham so that it forms a thin coat of transparent jelly resembling 'jade'. Allow to cool before serving.

MU SHU PORK WITH EGGS AND WOOD-EAR

Mu Shu Rou

Mu Shu is the Chinese name for a bright yellow flower. Traditionally, this dish is served as a filling wrapped in thin pancakes, but it can also be served on its own with plain rice.

SERVES 4

Ingredients
½oz dried wood-ear mushrooms
6–8oz pork tenderloin
8oz Napa cabbage
4oz bamboo shoots, drained
2 scallions
3 eggs
I tsp salt
4 tbsp vegetable oil
I tbsp light soy sauce
I tbsp Chinese rice wine or dry sherry
few drops sesame oil

1 Soak the fungus in cold water for 25–30 minutes, rinse, and discard the hard stalks, if any. Drain, then thinly shred.

2 Cut the pork into matchstick-size shreds. Thinly shred the Napa cabbage, bamboo shoots, and scallions.

3 Beat the eggs with a pinch of the salt and lightly scramble in a little of the warm oil until set, but not too dry. Remove.

4 Heat the remaining oil in the wok and stir-fry the pork for about 1 minute, or until the color changes.

5 Add the vegetables to the wok, stir-fry for 1 minute more, then add the remaining salt, the soy sauce, and wine or sherry.

6 Stir for 1 more minute before adding the scrambled eggs. Break up the scrambled eggs and blend well. Sprinkle with sesame oil and serve.

STUFFED GREEN BELL PEPPERS

Niang Qing Chaio

Ideally, use small, thin-skinned green bell peppers for this recipe.

SERVES 4

Ingredients
8–10oz ground pork
4–6 water chestnuts, finely chopped
2 scallions, finely chopped
½ tsp finely chopped fresh ginger
1 tbsp light soy sauce
1 tbsp Chinese rice wine or dry sherry
3–4 green bell peppers, cored and seeded

1 tbsp cornstarch
vegetable oil, for deep-frying

Sauce
2 tsp light soy sauce
1 tsp light brown sugar
1–2 fresh hot chilies, finely chopped (optional)
about 5 tbsp Basic Stock or water

1 In a bowl, combine the ground pork, water chestnuts, scallions, ginger, soy sauce, and wine or sherry, and mix thoroughly until blended.

2 Halve or quarter the green bell peppers. Stuff the sections with the pork mixture and sprinkle with a little cornstarch.

3 Heat the oil in a preheated wok and deep-fry the stuffed bell peppers, with the meat-side down, for 2–3 minutes, then remove and drain.

4 Pour off the excess oil, then return the stuffed green bell peppers to the wok with the meat-side up. Add the sauce ingredients, shaking the wok gently to make sure they do not stick to the bottom, and braise for 2–3 minutes. Carefully lift the stuffed peppers onto a serving dish, meat-side up, and pour the sauce over them. Serve.

Twice-cooked Pork – Sichuan Style

Hui Guo Rou

Any leftovers from a pork roast can be used for this dish.

SERVES 4

Ingredients
8oz pork shoulder
1 small green bell pepper, cored and seeded
4oz sliced bamboo shoots, rinsed and drained
1 scallion

3 tbsp vegetable oil
1 tsp salt
½ tsp light brown sugar
1 tbsp yellow bean sauce
1 tsp hot bean sauce
1 tbsp Chinese rice wine or dry sherry

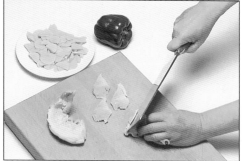

1 Immerse the whole piece of pork into a pot of boiling water, return to a boil, and skim the surface. Reduce the heat and simmer, covered, for 25–30 minutes. Turn off the heat and leave the pork in the water, covered, to cool, for at least 3–4 hours before removing.

2 Trim off and remove any excess fat from the pork and cut the meat into thin slices, each about the size of a large postage stamp. Cut the green bell peppers into pieces the size of the bamboo shoots and cut the scallion into short sections.

3 Heat the oil in a preheated wok, add the green bell pepper, the scallion, and bamboo shoots, and stir-fry for 1 minute.

4 Add the pork followed by the salt, sugar, yellow bean sauce, hot bean sauce, and wine or sherry. Continue stirring for 1–2 minutes more. Serve.

SWEET AND SOUR PORK

Tang Cu Gu Luo Rou

Sweet and Sour Pork must be one of the most popular dishes served in Chinese restaurants and take-outs in the Western world. Unfortunately, it is too often spoiled by cooks who use too much tomato ketchup in the sauce. Here is a classic recipe from Canton, the city of its origin.

SERVES 4

Ingredients
12oz lean pork
¼ tsp salt
½ tsp ground Sichuan peppercorns
1 tbsp Chinese rice wine or dry sherry
4oz bamboo shoots

2 tbsp all-purpose flour
1 egg, lightly beaten
vegetable oil, for deep-frying

Sauce
1 tbsp vegetable oil
1 clove garlic, finely chopped
1 scallion, cut into short sections

1 small green bell pepper, cut into small cubes
1 fresh red chili, seeded and thinly shredded
1 tbsp light soy sauce
2 tbsp light brown sugar
2–3 tbsp rice vinegar
1 tbsp tomato paste
about ½ cup Basic Stock or water

1 Cut the pork into small bite-sized cubes. Marinate with the salt, pepper, and wine or sherry for 15–20 minutes.

2 Cut the bamboo shoots into small cubes the same size as the pork.

3 Dust the pork with flour, dip in the beaten egg, and coat with more flour. Deep-fry in moderately hot oil for 3–4 minutes, stirring to separate the pieces. Remove.

4 Reheat the oil to hot, add the pork and bamboo shoots, and fry for about 1 minute or until golden. Remove and drain.

5 Heat the oil and add the garlic, scallion, green bell pepper and red chili. Stir-fry for 30–40 seconds, then add the seasoning with the stock. Bring to the boil, then add the pork and bamboo shoots.

STIR-FRIED PORK WITH VEGETABLES I

Rou Pian Chao Shucai

This is a basic recipe for cooking any meat with any vegetables, according to seasonal availability.

SERVES 4	1 tsp Chinese rice wine or dry sherry	4 tbsp vegetable oil
	2 tsp cornstarch paste	1 tsp salt
Ingredients	4oz snow peas	Basic Stock or water, if necessary
8oz pork tenderloin	4oz mushrooms	few drops sesame oil
1 tbsp light soy sauce	1 medium or 2 small carrots	
1 tsp light brown sugar	1 scallion	

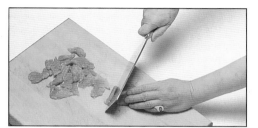

1 Cut the pork into thin slices each about the size of an oblong postage stamp. Marinate with about 1 tsp of the soy sauce, sugar, wine or sherry, and cornstarch paste.

2 Top and tail the snow peas; thinly slice the mushrooms; cut the carrots into pieces roughly the same size as the pork, and cut the scallion into short sections.

3 Heat the oil in a preheated wok and stir-fry the pork for about 1 minute or until its color changes. Remove with a slotted spoon and keep warm.

4 Stir-fry the vegetables for about 2 minutes, add the salt and the partly-cooked pork, and a little stock or water only if necessary. Continue stirring for 1–2 minutes more, then add the remaining soy sauce and blend. Sprinkle with sesame oil and serve.

LION'S HEAD CASSEROLE

Shi Zi Tou

The meatballs are supposed to resemble a lion's head, and the Napa cabbage its mane, hence this dish's name.

SERVES 4–6

Ingredients
1lb ground pork
2 tsp finely chopped scallions
1 tsp finely chopped fresh ginger

2oz mushrooms, finely chopped
2oz peeled shrimp or crabmeat, finely chopped
1 tbsp light soy sauce
1 tsp light brown sugar
1 tbsp Chinese rice wine or dry sherry
1 tbsp cornstarch

1½lb Napa cabbage
3–4 tbsp vegetable oil
1 tsp salt
about 1¼ cups Basic Stock or water

1 Mix the pork with the scallions, ginger, mushrooms, shrimp, soy sauce, sugar, wine, and cornstarch. Shape the mixture into 4–6 meatballs.

2 Cut the Napa cabbage into large pieces, all roughly the same size.

3 Heat the oil and stir-fry the Napa cabbage with the salt for 2–3 minutes. Add the meatballs and the stock, bring to a boil, cover and simmer gently for 30–45 minutes.

STIR-FRIED PORK WITH VEGETABLES II

Rou Pian Chao Shucai

In this simple, colorful dish, the zucchini can be replaced by cucumber or green bell peppers.

SERVES 4

Ingredients
8oz pork tenderloin, thinly sliced
1 tbsp light soy sauce

1 tsp light brown sugar
1 tsp Chinese rice wine or dry sherry
2 tsp cornstarch paste
4oz firm tomatoes, peeled
6oz zucchini

1 scallion
4 tbsp vegetable oil
1 tsp salt (optional)
Basic Stock or water, if necessary

1 In a bowl, marinate with the pork about 1 tsp of the soy sauce, the sugar, wine, and cornstarch paste. Cut the tomatoes and zucchini into wedges and the scallion into sections.

2 Heat the oil in a preheated wok and stir-fry the pork for about 1 minute or until the color changes. Remove with a slotted spoon and keep warm.

3 Stir-fry the vegetables for 2–3 minutes, add the salt if using, the pork, and a little stock or water. Stir for 1 minute more or so, then add the remaining soy sauce. Serve.

SWEET AND SOUR LAMB

Tang Cu Yang Rou

This recipe from the Imperial kitchens of the Manchu Dynasty is perhaps a forerunner of Sweet and Sour Pork.

SERVES 4	vegetable oil, for deep-frying	2 tbsp rice vinegar
	½ tsp finely chopped fresh ginger	2 tbsp light brown sugar
Ingredients	½ hothouse cucumber, thinly sliced	3–4 tbsp Basic Stock or water
12–14oz boneless leg of lamb	1 tbsp light soy sauce	1 tbsp cornstarch paste
1 tbsp yellow bean sauce	1 tbsp Chinese rice wine or dry sherry	½ tsp sesame oil

1 Cut the lamb into thin slices each about the size of an oblong postage stamp. In a bowl, marinate the lamb with the yellow bean sauce for 35–40 minutes.

2 In a wok, deep-fry the lamb in the hot oil for about 30–40 seconds or until the color changes. Remove with a slotted spoon and drain well.

3 Pour off the excess oil, leaving about ½ tbsp in the wok. Add the ginger and the remaining ingredients and stir until smooth. Add the lamb, blend well, and serve.

STIR-FRIED LAMB WITH SCALLIONS

Cong Bao Yang Rou

This is a classic Beijing recipe, in which the lamb can be replaced with either beef or pork, and the scallions by other strongly flavored vegetables, such as leeks or onions.

SERVES 4	1 tbsp light soy sauce	about 1¼ cups vegetable oil
	1 tbsp Chinese rice wine or dry sherry	few small pieces fresh ginger
Ingredients	2 tsp cornstarch paste	2 tbsp yellow bean sauce
12–14 oz boneless leg of lamb	½oz dried wood-ear mushrooms	few drops sesame oil
1 tsp light brown sugar	6–8 scallions	

1 Slice the lamb thinly. Marinate with the sugar, soy sauce, wine, and cornstarch paste for 30–45 minutes. Soak the mushrooms for 25–30 minutes, then cut into small pieces with the scallions.

2 Heat the oil in a preheated wok until hot and stir-fry the meat for about 1 minute, or until the color changes. Remove with a slotted spoon and drain.

3 Keep about 1 tbsp of oil in the wok, then add the scallions, ginger, mushrooms, and yellow bean sauce. Blend well, add the meat, and stir for about 1 minute. Sprinkle with the sesame oil.

DRY-FRIED SHREDDED BEEF

Gan Shao Niu Rou

Dry-frying is a unique Sichuan cooking method, in which the main ingredient is first stir-fried slowly over a low heat until dry, then finished off quickly with other ingredients over a high heat.

SERVES 4

Ingredients
12–14oz lean beef
1 large or 2 small carrots
2–3 stalks celery
2 tbsp sesame oil
1 tbsp Chinese rice wine or dry sherry

1 tbsp hot bean sauce
1 tbsp light soy sauce
1 clove garlic, finely chopped
1 tsp light brown sugar
2–3 scallions, finely chopped
½ tsp finely chopped fresh ginger
ground Sichuan peppercorns, to taste

1 Cut the beef into matchstick-size strips. Thinly shred the carrots and celery.

2 Heat the sesame oil in a preheated wok (it will smoke very quickly). Reduce the heat and stir-fry the beef shreds with the wine or sherry until the color changes.

3 Pour off the excess liquid and reserve. Continue stirring until the meat is absolutely dry.

4 Add the hot bean sauce, soy sauce, garlic, and sugar. Blend well, then add the carrot and celery shreds. Increase the heat to high and add the scallions, ginger, and the reserved liquid. Continue stirring, and when all the juice has evaporated, season with Sichuan pepper and serve.

BEEF WITH CANTONESE OYSTER SAUCE

Hao You Niu Rou

This is a classic Cantonese recipe in which any combination of vegetables can be used. Broccoli can be used instead of snow peas, bamboo shoots instead of baby corn, and ordinary mushrooms instead of straw mushrooms, for example.

SERVES 4

Ingredients
10–12oz lean beef
1 tsp light brown sugar
1 tbsp light soy sauce
2 tsp Chinese rice wine or dry sherry
2 tsp cornstarch paste

4oz snow peas
4oz baby corn
4oz canned straw mushrooms, drained
1 scallion
1¼ cups vegetable oil
few small pieces fresh ginger
½ tsp salt
2 tbsp oyster sauce

1 Cut the beef into thin slices each about the size of an oblong postage stamp. In a bowl, marinate the beef with the sugar, soy sauce, wine or sherry, and cornstarch paste for 25–30 minutes.

2 Top and tail the snow peas; cut the baby corn in half and also the straw mushrooms if large, but leave whole if small. Cut the scallion into short sections.

3 Heat the oil in a preheated wok and stir-fry the beef until the color changes. Remove with a slotted spoon and drain.

4 Pour off the excess oil, leaving about 2 tbsp in the wok, then add the scallion, ginger, and the vegetables. Stir-fry for about 2 minutes with the salt, then add the beef and the oyster sauce. Blend well and serve.

STIR-FRIED MIXED VEGETABLES I

Su Shi Jin

Black or oyster mushrooms may be used in place of the ordinary mushrooms in this dish.

SERVES 4	4oz mushrooms	Basic Stock or water, if necessary
	1 medium red bell pepper, cored and seeded	1 tbsp light soy sauce
Ingredients	4 tbsp vegetable oil	few drops sesame oil (optional)
4oz snow peas	1 tsp salt	
4oz zucchini	1 tsp light brown sugar	

1 Cut the vegetables into similar shapes and sizes. Top and tail the snow peas and leave whole if small, otherwise cut in half.

2 Heat the oil in a wok and stir-fry the vegetables for about 2 minutes.

3 Add the salt and sugar, and a little stock or water *only* if necessary, and stir for 1 minute. Finally add the soy sauce and sesame oil, if using. Blend well and serve.

STIR-FRIED MIXED VEGETABLES II

Su Shi Jin

When selecting different items for a dish, never mix ingredients indiscriminately. The idea is to achieve a harmonious balance of color and texture.

SERVES 4	4oz broccoli	Basic Stock or water, if necessary
	1 medium or 2 small carrots	1 tbsp light soy sauce
Ingredients	4 tbsp vegetable oil	few drops sesame oil (optional)
8oz Napa cabbage	1 tsp salt	
4oz baby corn	1 tsp light brown sugar	

1 Cut the vegetables into roughly similar shapes and sizes.

2 Heat the oil in a wok and stir-fry the vegetables for about 2 minutes.

3 Add the salt and sugar, and a little stock or water *only* if necessary, and continue stirring for another minute. Add the soy sauce and sesame oil, if using. Blend well and serve.

SICHUAN SPICY TOFU

Ma Po Dao Fu

This universally popular dish originated in Sichuan in the nineteenth century. The meat used in the recipe can be omitted to create a purely vegetarian dish.

SERVES 4

Ingredients
3 cakes tofu
1 leek
4 oz ground beef
3 tbsp vegetable oil
1 tbsp black bean sauce

1 tbsp light soy sauce
1 tsp hot bean sauce
1 tbsp Chinese rice wine or dry sherry
about 3–4 tbsp Basic Stock or water
2 tsp cornstarch paste
ground Sichuan peppercorns, to taste
few drops sesame oil

1 Cut the tofu into ½in square cubes. Blanch the cubes in a pan of boiling water for 2–3 minutes to harden. Remove and drain. Cut the leek into short sections.

2 Stir-fry the ground beef in oil until the color changes, then add the leek and black bean sauce. Add the tofu with the soy sauce, hot bean sauce, and wine or sherry. Stir gently for 1 minute.

3 Add the stock or water, bring to a boil, and braise for 2–3 minutes.

4 Thicken the sauce with the cornstarch paste, season with the ground Sichuan pepper, and sprinkle with the sesame oil.

Yu Hsiang Eggplant in Spicy Sauce

Yu Hsiang Gai

Y*u Hsiang*, which literally means 'fish fragrance', is a Sichuan term indicating that the dish is cooked with seasonings originally used in fish dishes.

SERVES 4

Ingredients
1lb eggplant
3–4 whole dried red chilies, soaked in water
 for 10 minutes
vegetable oil, for deep-frying
1 clove garlic, finely chopped

1 tsp finely chopped fresh ginger
1 tsp finely chopped scallions, white part only
4oz lean pork, thinly sliced (optional)
1 tbsp light soy sauce
1 tsp light brown sugar
1 tbsp hot bean sauce
1 tbsp Chinese rice wine or dry sherry
1 tbsp rice vinegar

2 tsp cornstarch paste
1 tsp finely chopped scallions, green part only,
 to garnish
few drops sesame oil

1 Cut the eggplant into short strips the size of French fries – the skin can either be peeled or left on, whichever you prefer. Cut the soaked red chilies into 2–3 small pieces and discard the seeds.

2 In a wok, heat the oil and deep-fry the eggplant 'fries' for about 3–4 minutes or until limp. Remove and drain.

3 Pour off the excess oil, leaving about 1 tbsp in the wok. Add the garlic, ginger, scallion whites, and chilies, stir a few times then add the pork, if using. Stir-fry the meat for about 1 minute or until the color changes to pale white. Add all the seasonings, then bring to a boil.

4 Add the eggplant to the wok, blend well, and braise for 30–40 seconds, then thicken the sauce with the cornstarch paste, stirring until smooth. Garnish with the scallion greens and sprinkle with the sesame oil.

Cook's tip

Soaking dried chilies in water will reduce their spicy flavor. If you prefer a milder chili taste, soak for longer than the recommended 10 minutes.

BROCCOLI IN OYSTER SAUCE

Hao You Xi Lan

Vegetarians may prefer to replace oyster sauce with soy sauce.

SERVES 4

Ingredients
1lb broccoli
3–4 tbsp vegetable oil
½ tsp salt
½ tsp light brown sugar
2–3 tbsp Basic Stock or water
2 tbsp oyster sauce

1 Cut the broccoli heads into florets; remove the rough skin from the stalks, and diagonally slice the florets into diamond-shaped chunks.

2 Heat the oil in a preheated wok and add the salt, then stir-fry the broccoli for about 2 minutes. Add the sugar, and stock or water, and continue stirring for another minute. Finally add the oyster sauce, blend well, and serve.

STIR-FRIED NAPA CABBAGE WITH MUSHROOMS

Pia Cai Cao Gu

You can also use fresh button mushrooms for this recipe.

SERVES 4

Ingredients
8oz fresh straw mushrooms or 12oz can straw mushrooms, drained
4 tbsp vegetable oil
14 oz Napa cabbage, cut in strips
1 tsp salt
1 tsp light brown sugar
1 tbsp cornstarch paste
½ cup milk

1 Cut the mushrooms in half lengthwise. Heat half the oil, stir-fry the Napa cabbage for 2 minutes, then add half the salt and half the sugar. Stir for 1 minute, then place on a dish.

2 Stir-fry the mushrooms for 1 minute. Add salt and sugar, cook for 1 minute, then thicken with the cornstarch paste and milk. Serve with the cabbage.

STIR-FRIED BEAN SPROUTS

Chao Dao Ya

It is not necessary to top and tail the bean sprouts for this quick and simple recipe. Simply rinse in a bowl of cold water, and discard any husks that float to the surface.

SERVES 4

Ingredients
2–3 scallions
8oz fresh bean sprouts
3 tbsp vegetable oil
1 tsp salt
½ tsp light brown sugar
few drops sesame oil (optional)

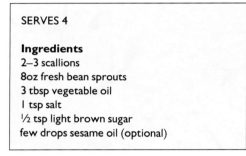

1 Cut the scallions into short sections about the same length as the bean sprouts.

2 Heat the oil in a wok and stir-fry the bean sprouts and scallions for about 1 minute. Add the salt and sugar and continue stirring for another minute. Sprinkle with the sesame oil, if using, and serve. Do not overcook, or the sprouts will go soggy.

BRAISED CHINESE VEGETABLES

Lo Han Zhai

The original recipe calls for no less than 18 different ingredients to represent the 18 Buddhas (*Lo Han*). Later, this was reduced to eight, but nowadays anything between four and six items is regarded as more than sufficient.

SERVES 4

Ingredients
¼oz dried wood-ear mushrooms
3oz straw mushrooms, drained
3oz sliced bamboo shoots, drained
2oz snow peas
1 cake tofu
6oz Napa cabbage

3–4 tbsp vegetable oil
1 tsp salt
½ tsp light brown sugar
1 tbsp light soy sauce
few drops sesame oil (optional)

1 Soak the wood ear mushrooms in cold water for 20–25 minutes, then rinse and discard the hard stalks, if any. Cut the straw mushrooms in half lengthwise, if large, cut in pieces, if small, keep them whole. Rinse and drain the bamboo shoot slices. Top and tail the snow peas. Cut the tofu into about 12 small pieces. Cut the cabbage into small pieces about the same size as the snow peas.

2 Harden the tofu pieces by placing them in a pan of boiling water for about 2 minutes. Remove and drain.

3 Heat the oil in a flameproof casserole or saucepan and lightly brown the tofu pieces on both sides. Remove with a slotted spoon and keep warm.

4 Stir-fry all the vegetables in the casserole or saucepan for about 1½ minutes, then add the tofu pieces, salt, sugar, and soy sauce. Continue stirring for another minute, then cover and braise for 2–3 minutes. Sprinkle with sesame oil (if using) and serve.

BAMBOO SHOOTS AND CHINESE MUSHROOMS

Chao Shang Dong

Another name for this dish is 'Twin Winter Vegetables', because both the bamboo shoots and mushrooms are at their best during the winter. For that reason, try using canned winter bamboo shoots and extra 'fat' mushrooms.

SERVES 4	10oz winter bamboo shoots	1 tbsp Chinese rice wine or dry sherry
	3 tbsp vegetable oil	½ tsp light brown sugar
Ingredients	1 scallion, cut into short sections	2 tsp cornstarch paste
2oz dried Chinese mushrooms (shiitake)	2 tbsp light soy sauce or oyster sauce	few drops sesame oil

1 Soak the mushrooms in cold water for at least 3 hours, then squeeze dry and discard any hard stalks, reserving the water. Cut the mushrooms in half, or quarters if they are large – keep them whole if small.

2 Rinse and drain the bamboo shoots, then cut into small, wedge-shaped pieces.

3 Heat the oil in a preheated wok and stir-fry the mushrooms and bamboo shoots for about 1 minute. Add the scallion and seasonings with about 2–3 tbsp of the mushroom water. Bring to the boil and braise for 1–2 more minutes, then thicken the gravy with the cornstarch paste and sprinkle with the sesame oil.

STIR-FRIED TOMATOES, CUCUMBER, AND EGGS

Chao San Wei

The cucumber can be replaced by a green bell pepper or zucchini if preferred.

SERVES 4	⅓ hothouse cucumber, unpeeled	4 tbsp vegetable oil
	4 eggs	2 tsp Chinese rice wine or dry sherry (optional)
Ingredients	1 tsp salt	
6oz firm tomatoes, peeled	1 scallion, finely chopped	

1 Halve the tomatoes and cucumber, then cut across into small wedges. In a bowl, beat the eggs with a pinch of the salt and a few pieces of the scallion.

2 Heat about half of the oil in a preheated wok, then lightly scramble the eggs over a moderate heat until set, but not too dry. Remove and keep warm.

3 Heat the remaining oil over a high heat, add the vegetables, and stir-fry for 1 minute. Add the remaining salt, then the scrambled eggs, and wine or sherry, if using.

NOODLES IN SOUP

Tang Mein

In China, noodles in soup (*Tang Mein*) are far more popular than Fried Noodles (*Chow Mein*). This is a basic recipe that you can adapt by using different ingredients for the 'dressing'.

SERVES 4

Ingredients
8oz boneless chicken breast, pork tenderloin, or
   pre-cooked meat
3–4 Chinese dried mushrooms (shiitake), soaked
4oz sliced bamboo shoots, drained
4oz spinach leaves, lettuce hearts, or Napa
   cabbage
2 scallions
12oz dried egg noodles
2½ cups Basic Stock
2 tbsp vegetable oil
1 tsp salt
½ tsp light brown sugar
1 tbsp light soy sauce

2 tsp Chinese rice wine or dry sherry
few drops sesame oil

1 Thinly shred the meat. Squeeze dry the mushrooms and discard any hard stalks. Thinly shred the mushrooms, bamboo shoots, greens, and scallions.

2 Cook the noodles in boiling water according to the instructions on the packet, then drain and rinse under cold water. Place in a serving bowl.

3 Bring the stock to a boil and pour over the noodles; keep warm.

4 Heat the oil in a preheated wok, add about half of the scallions and the meat, and stir-fry for about 1 minute.

5 Add the mushrooms, bamboo shoots, and greens, and stir-fry for 1 minute. Add all the seasonings and blend well.

6 Pour the 'dressing' over the noodles, garnish with the remaining scallions, and serve immediately.

PLAIN RICE

Pai Fan

Use long-grain or patna rice, or fragrant rice from Thailand. Allow ⅓ cup uncooked rice per person.

SERVES 4	1 cup cold water
	pinch of salt
Ingredients	½ tsp vegetable oil
1 ⅓ cups rice	

1 Wash and rinse the rice. Place the rice in a saucepan and add the water. There should be no more than ⅔in of water above the surface of the rice.

2 Bring to a boil, add the salt, and oil, then stir to prevent the rice sticking to the bottom of the pan. Reduce the heat to very, very low and cook for 15–20 minutes, covered.

3 Remove from the heat and leave to stand for 10 minutes. Fluff up the rice with a fork or spoon just before serving.

EGG FRIED RICE

Dan Chao Fan

Use rice with a fairly firm texture. Ideally, the rice should be soaked in water for a short time before cooking.

SERVES 4	2–3 tbsp vegetable oil
	1lb cooked rice
Ingredients	4oz green peas
3 eggs	
1 tsp salt	
2 scallions, finely chopped	

1 In a bowl, lightly beat the eggs with a pinch of the salt and a few pieces of scallion.

2 Heat the oil in a preheated wok, and lightly scramble the eggs.

3 Add the rice and stir to make sure that each grain of rice is separated. Add the remaining salt, scallions, and the peas. Blend well and serve.

PORK DUMPLINGS

Jiao Zi

These dumplings make a good starter to a multi-course meal when shallow-fried. They can also be served on their own as a snack, if steamed, or as a complete meal when poached in large quantities.

MAKES ABOUT 80–90 DUMPLINGS

Ingredients
4 cups all-purpose flour
about 2 cups water
flour, for dusting

Filling
1lb Napa white cabbage
1lb ground pork
1 tbsp finely chopped scallions
1 tsp finely chopped fresh ginger
2 tsp salt
1 tsp light brown sugar
2 tbsp light soy sauce
1 tbsp Chinese rice wine or dry sherry
2 tsp sesame oil

Dipping Sauce

2 tbsp red chili oil
1 tbsp light soy sauce
1 tsp finely chopped garlic
1 tbsp finely chopped scallions

Combine all the ingredients in a small bowl, and serve with Pork Dumplings.

1 Sift the flour into a bowl, then slowly pour in the water and mix to a firm dough. Knead until smooth and soft, then cover with a damp cloth and set aside for 25–30 minutes.

2 For the filling, blanch the cabbage leaves in boiling water until soft. Drain and chop finely. Mix the cabbage with the remaining ingredients.

3 Lightly dust a work surface with flour. Knead and roll the dough into a long sausage about 1in in diameter. Cut the 'sausage' into about 80–90 small pieces and flatten each piece with the palm of your hand.

4 Using a rolling pin, roll out each piece into a thin pancake about 2.5in in diameter.

5 Place about 1½ tbsp of the filling in the center of each pancake and fold into a half-moon-shaped pouch.

6 Pinch the edges firmly so that the dumpling is tightly sealed.

Shallow-frying: Heat 3 tbsp of oil in a wok or frying pan. Place the dumplings in rows in the oil and fry over a medium heat for 2–3 minutes.

Steaming: Place the dumplings on a bed of lettuce leaves on the rack of a bamboo steamer and steam for 10–12 minutes on a high heat. Serve hot with a dipping sauce.

Poaching: Cook the dumplings in about ⅔ cup salted boiling water for 2 minutes. Remove from the heat, and leave the dumplings in the water for about 15 minutes.

SPECIAL FRIED RICE

Yangchow Chao Fan

Special Fried Rice is more elaborate than Egg Fried Rice, and almost a meal in itself.

SERVES 4

Ingredients
2oz peeled and cooked shrimp
2oz cooked ham
4oz green peas
3 eggs
1 tsp salt
2 scallions, finely chopped
4 tbsp vegetable oil
1 tbsp light soy sauce
1 tbsp Chinese rice wine or dry sherry
1lb cooked rice

1 Pat dry the shrimp with paper towels. Cut the ham into small dice about the same size as the peas.

2 In a bowl, lightly beat the eggs with a pinch of the salt and a few pieces of the scallions.

3 Heat about half of the oil in a preheated wok, stir-fry the peas, shrimp, and ham for 1 minute, then add the soy sauce and wine or sherry. Remove and keep warm.

4 Heat the remaining oil in the wok and lightly scramble the eggs. Add the rice and stir to make sure that each grain of rice is separated. Add the remaining salt, scallions, shrimp, ham, and peas. Blend well and serve either hot or cold.

WONTON SOUP

Wun Tun Tang

In China, wonton soup is served as a snack or Dim Sum rather than as a soup course during a large meal.

SERVES 4

Ingredients
6oz pork, not too lean, coarsely chopped
2oz peeled shrimp, finely chopped
1 tsp light brown sugar
1 tbsp Chinese rice wine or dry sherry
1 tbsp light soy sauce
1 tsp finely chopped scallions
1 tsp finely chopped fresh ginger
24 ready-made wonton skins
about 3 cups Basic Stock
1 tbsp light soy sauce
finely chopped scallions, to garnish

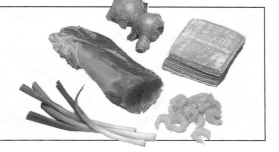

1 In a bowl, mix the pork and shrimp with the sugar, wine or sherry, soy sauce, scallions, and ginger. Blend well and leave to stand for 25–30 minutes.

2 Place about 1 tsp of the filling at the center of each wonton skin.

3 Wet and join the edges of each wonton, pressing down with your fingers to seal, then fold each wonton over.

4 To cook, bring the stock to a rolling boil in a wok or saucepan, add the wontons and cook for 4–5 minutes. Season with the soy sauce and garnish with the scallions. Serve.

SEAFOOD CHOW MEIN

Hai Wei Chao Mein

This basic recipe can be adapted using different items for the 'dressing'.

SERVES 4

Ingredients
3oz squid, cleaned
3oz uncooked shrimp
3–4 fresh scallops
½ egg white
1 tbsp cornstarch paste
9oz egg noodles
5–6 tbsp vegetable oil
2oz snow peas
½ tsp salt

½ tsp light brown sugar
1 tbsp Chinese rice wine or dry sherry
2 tbsp light soy sauce
2 scallions, finely shredded
Basic Stock, if necessary
few drops sesame oil

1 Open up the squid and, using a sharp knife, score the inside in a criss-cross pattern. Cut the squid into pieces each about the size of a postage stamp. Soak the squid in a bowl of boiling water until all the pieces curl up. Rinse in cold water and drain.

2 Peel the shrimp and cut each in half lengthwise.

3 Cut each scallop into 3–4 slices. Mix the scallops and shrimp with the egg white and cornstarch paste.

4 Cook the noodles in boiling water according to the instructions on the packet, then drain and rinse under cold water. Mix with about 1 tbsp of the oil.

5 Heat about 2–3 tbsp of the oil in a wok until hot. Stir-fry the snow peas and seafood for about 2 minutes then add the salt, sugar, wine or sherry, half of the soy sauce, and about half of the scallions. Blend well and add a little stock if necessary. Remove and keep warm.

6 Heat the remaining oil in the wok and stir-fry the noodles for 2–3 minutes with the remaining soy sauce. Place in a large serving dish, pour the 'dressing' on top, garnish with the remaining scallions, and sprinkle with sesame oil. Serve hot or cold.

DESSERTS

THIN PANCAKES

Bao Bing

Thin pancakes are not too difficult to make, but quite a lot of practice and patience is needed to achieve the perfect result. Nowadays, even restaurants buy frozen ready-made ones from Chinese supermarkets. If you decide to use ready-made pancakes, or are reheating homemade ones, steam them for about 5 minutes, or microwave on high (650 watts) for 1–2 minutes.

MAKES 24–30	about 1¼ cups boiling water	*Cook's tip*
Ingredients	1 tsp vegetable oil	Cooked pancakes can be stored in the refrigerator for several days.
4 cups all-purpose flour	flour, for dusting	

1 Sift the flour into a mixing bowl, then pour in the boiling water very gently, stirring as you pour. Mix with the oil and knead the mixture into a firm dough. Cover this with a damp towel and let stand for about 30 minutes. Lightly dust a work surface with flour.

2 Knead the dough for about 5–8 minutes or until smooth, then divide it into 3 equal portions. Roll out each portion into a long 'sausage', cut each into 8–10 pieces, and roll each into a ball. Using your palm, press each piece into a flat pancake. With a rolling pin, gently roll each into a 6in circle.

3 Heat an ungreased frying pan until hot, then reduce the heat to low and place the pancakes, one at a time, in the pan. Remove the pancakes when small brown spots appear on the underside. Keep under a damp cloth until all the pancakes are cooked.

RED BEAN PASTE PANCAKES

Hong Dao Guo Ping

If you are unable to find red bean paste, sweetened chestnut purée or mashed dates are possible substitutes.

SERVES 4	8 Thin Pancakes	
	2–3 tbsp vegetable oil	
Ingredients	granulated or superfine sugar, to serve	
about 8 tbsp sweetened red bean paste		

1 Spread about 1 tbsp of the red bean paste over about three-quarters of each pancake, then roll each pancake over three or four times.

2 Heat the oil in a wok or frying pan and shallow-fry the pancake rolls until golden brown, turning once.

3 Cut each pancake roll into 3–4 pieces and sprinkle with sugar to serve.

TOFFEE APPLES

Ba Tsu Ping Guo

A variety of fruits, such as banana and pineapple, can be prepared and cooked the same way.

SERVES 4

Ingredients
4 firm eating apples, peeled and cored
1 cup all-purpose flour
about ½ cup cold water
1 egg, beaten

vegetable oil, for deep-frying, plus 2 tbsp for the toffee
½ cup granulated or superfine sugar

1 Cut each apple into 8 pieces. Dust each piece with a little of the flour.

2 Sift the remaining flour into a mixing bowl, then slowly add the cold water and stir to make a smooth batter. Add the beaten egg and blend well.

3 Heat the oil in a wok. Dip the apple pieces in the batter and deep-fry for about 3 minutes or until golden. Remove and drain.

4 Heat 2 tbsp of the oil in the wok, add the sugar and stir continuously until the sugar has caramelized. Quickly add the apple pieces and blend well so that each piece of apple is coated with the 'toffee'. Dip the apple pieces in cold water to harden before serving.

ALMOND FLOAT

Xing Ren Tou Fou

This light and simple dessert is usually made from agar-agar or isinglass, though gelatin can also be used.

SERVES 4–6

Ingredients
¼oz agar-agar or isinglass or 1oz
   gelatin powder
about 2½ cups water
4 tbsp granulated or superfine sugar

1¼ cups milk
1 tsp almond extract
fresh or canned mixed fruit salad with syrup, to
   serve

1 In a saucepan, dissolve the agar-agar or isinglass in about half of the water over a gentle heat. This will take at least 10 minutes. If using gelatin, follow the instructions.

2 In a separate saucepan, dissolve the sugar in the remaining water over a medium heat. Add the milk and the almond extract, blending well, but do not boil.

3 Mix the milk and sugar with the agar-agar or isinglass mixture (or gelatin, if using) in a large serving bowl. When cool, place in the refrigerator for 2–3 hours to set.

4 To serve, cut the almond mixture into small cubes and spoon into a serving dish or into individual bowls. Pour the fruit salad, with the syrup, over the cubes and serve.

TASTE OF ASIA

STEVEN WHEELER

The cooking of Southeast Asia provides a fascinating glimpse of its people and way of life. This section includes recipes from Thailand, Vietnam, Malaysia, Singapore, Indonesia, the Philippines, and Japan and the dishes reveal how each country has established its own style of eating. Characteristics vary among the three main religions – Muslim, Buddhist and Christian – but it is accepted by all that ingredients must be fresh and full of flavor. It is this commitment to perfect ingredients that puts life into much of the cooking of these regions. With such a wide variety of produce now available in Western supermarkets, there is every opportunity to explore a new side to our own cooking.

THE PRINCIPLES OF SOUTHEAST ASIAN COOKING

The cuisines of the countries of Southeast Asia vary considerably, from the Spanish-influenced dishes of the Philippines to the dietary demands of the Buddhist and Muslim faiths. One practice common to most countries is the method of serving. Mealtimes are relaxed, informal affairs, with all dishes arriving at the table at the same time. Guests help themselves, either with chopsticks or by hand. Dishes should offer a balance of textures and aromas, and ingredients must be fresh and flavorsome.

EQUIPMENT AND UTENSILS

Bamboo skewers (1) Bamboo skewers are widely used for barbecues and broiled foods. They are disposed of after use.

Chopping board (2) It is worth investing in a solid chopping board. Thick boards provide the best surface and will last for many years.

Citrus zesting tool (3) The outer peel or zest of citrus fruit imparts a distinctive flavor to many Southeast Asian dishes. This tool is designed to remove the zest while leaving behind the bitter white pith of the fruit.

Cleavers (4, 5) At first sight cleavers may look and feel out of place for domestic use, but they are ideally suited to fine chopping and transferring ingredients from chopping board to wok. Small cleavers are used mostly for chopping and shredding fruits and vegetables. They can also be used for the preparation of meat and fish.

Cooking chopsticks (6) Extra long chopsticks can be used to stir ingredients in the wok. Their length permits you to keep at a distance from the cooking ingredients.

Draining wire (7) Draining wires are designed to rest on the side of a wok. They are used mainly for deep-frying.

Food processor (8) The food processor is a useful alternative to the more traditional pestle and mortar, and is suitable for grinding wet spices.

Large chopping knife (9) If you are not comfortable using a cleaver, a large Western-style chopping knife can be used instead. Choose one with a deep blade to give you the best control.

Rice paddle (10) These are generally made from a large section of bamboo. Rice paddles are used to stir and fluff rice after cooking. A pair of chopsticks can also be used for fluffing rice.

Rice saucepan and lid (11) A good rice saucepan with a close-fitting lid is an essential piece of equipment for Southeast Asian cooking. Stainless steel pans with a heavy base are best.

Sharpening stone (12) Sharpening stones are used for sharpening knives and cleavers. They are available from kitchenware or hardware stores and should be immersed in water before use.

Stainless steel skimmer (13) Stainless steel skimmers should be used when strong flavors are likely to affect bare metal utensils.

Wire skimmer (14) Wire skimmers are used to retrieve cooked food from boiling water or hot fat. Bare metal skimmers can retain strong flavors and are therefore not recommended for use with fish-based liquids.

Wok (15) The wok is used in all parts of Southeast Asia. The shape of the wok allows deep-frying and stir-frying in a minimum of fat, thus retaining the freshness and flavor of ingredients.

Wok ladle (16) Wok ladles are used to stir liquid ingredients while cooking. They are also useful for transferring cooked food to serving bowls.

Wok lid (17) Wok lids have a large domed surface and are designed to retain moisture given off during cooking. The steam held beneath the lid is often used to keep ingredients from taking on too much color when frying.

Wok scoop (18) The wok scoop is designed to make contact with the curved surface of the wok. Most scoops are made of stainless steel and will not retain strong flavors.

INGREDIENTS

Acorn squash (1) Many varieties of squash and pumpkin are grown in Southeast Asia. They are used mainly as a vegetable, but may sometimes be used in desserts.

Banana leaves (3) The banana leaf is widely used for wrapping ingredients before cooking. If banana leaves are unavailable use aluminium foil.

Bean thread noodles (5) These fine noodles are usually made from mung bean flour, although some varieties contain rice, soy, and pea starch. When boiled, they have a smooth texture and are an important ingredient for spring roll stuffings. Bean thread noodles become crispy when deep-fried.

Cardamom pods (4) Cardamom is a member of the ginger family. The sweetest flavor is contained in the seed of the olive-green pods and is usually ground with other spices. Large black pods have a bitter flavor and combine well with sweet curry ingredients.

Chilies (6) Used in moderation, chilies provide the hot sweet glow typical of many Southeast Asian curries and dipping sauces. As a rule, small chilies are the hottest and green varieties tend to be less sweet than red.

Chinese red onions (shallots) (7) The Chinese red onion has a strong flavour despite its small size. If unavailable, use golden shallots or an increased quantity of white onions.

Cilantro (10) Fresh cilantro has a strong, pungent smell that combines well with other rich flavours. The white cilantro root is used when the green coloring is not required. Bunches of cilantro will keep for up to five days in a jar of water. Cover with a plastic bag and store in the refrigerator.

Cinnamon (cassia) (8) Tightly-curled cinnamon has a smooth, warm flavor which is given to sweet and savoury cooking. Cassia, pictured here, has a more robust flavor and is used with other strong spices.

Coconut (9) The coconut is essential to many dishes of Southeast Asia. Coconut milk is obtained from the white flesh of the nut and is both rich and smooth-tasting.

Coriander seeds (11) Coriander is common to all styles of cooking throughout Southeast Asia. The seeds are dry-fried with other spices to release the unique flavor.

Cumin seeds (12) Cumin has a similar ribbed shape to fennel seed and comes from the parsley family. It has a warm, heady flavor that combines

well with cilantro and is widely used in beef dishes. Cumin seeds are usually dry-fried before use.

Egg noodles (13) Egg noodles are made from wheat flour and are sold dried in single portions. When cooked, egg noodles are used in dishes such as Mee Goreng from Singapore and Pansit Guisado from the Philippines.

Egg plant (2) The dark-skinned egg plant is included in a variety of slow-cooking dishes and is renowned for its smooth texture. Large egg plant can be bitter and should be salted before use.

Enoki mushrooms (14) These slender mushrooms have a sweet, peppery taste and are used to enhance the clear broths of Japan. Enoki can also be eaten raw as a salad ingredient.

Fennel seeds (15) Plump green fennel seeds are similar in character to cumin, and have a sweet aniseed flavor. The seeds combine well with peanuts and the zest of citrus fruit, and are an aid to digestion.

Fermented shrimp paste (Blachan, Kapi) (16) The smell of fermented shrimp paste by itself is quite repellent, but when blended with other spices, shrimp paste loses its unpleasant flavor and provides the unique taste and character typical of many Southeast Asian sauces.

Galingal (17) Galingal is a member of the ginger family and grows in a similar root shape. The fibrous root has a resinous quality similar to pine and combines well with fish dishes. Dried galingal is increasingly available. It should be soaked in boiling water before use.

Garlic (18) Garlic marries well with the strong pungent flavors of the East. Individual cloves can be finely chopped or crushed in a garlic press.

Ginger (19) Fresh ginger is well known in the West for its warm, pungent flavor. In its native region of Southeast Asia, it features in many intriguing spice combinations.

Lime leaves (20) Lime leaves are an essential part of many slow-cooking dishes. The deep, citrus flavor of the leaf combines especially well with rich coconut milk and hot chili spices.

Limes (21) Limes are widely used to add sharpness to finished dishes. Wedges are often served at the table so that guests may season dishes to taste.

Lemon grass (22) Fresh lemon grass is common to many dishes throughout Southeast Asia. Its flavor has a rich lemon quality that combines well with other wet spices. Lemon grass is also available dried.

Lychees (23) The brittle skin of this fine fruit peels away like the shell of a boiled egg. The white, scented fruit has a clean fresh taste and is served at the end of a meal.

Mandarin oranges (24) The flavor obtained from the outer zest of the mandarin orange combines well with the rich spices of the East. Satsumas and clementines are also suitable.

Mango (25) The mango offers a rich scented flavor to both sweet and savory dishes. Mangoes are ripe when the green skin is flushed with red.

Mint (26) Varieties of mint feature in the cooking of Vietnam. The fresh flavor combines particularly well with cilantro, peanuts, and the zest of mandarin orange. Mint is also used in sweet and savory fruit salads.

Moolie (27) The giant white radish is common to many Japanese dishes and is ideal for making flower garnishes. If unavailable, white turnip or red radish can be substituted.

Nutmeg (28) The flavor of nutmeg is obtained by grating the nut on a fine grater. The fresh oils that are released provide strength and character to many well-known spice mixtures.

Pickled ginger (29) Thinly sliced pink pickled ginger is served as a condiment with Japanese sushi, grilled fish, and beef. It has a warm, sweet flavor and is found in most oriental food stores.

Pineapple (30) Pineapple offers a clean refreshing flavor and is an aid to digestion. It may be served at the end of a meal, or as an ingredient in a main dish.

Scallions (36) Scallions have a milder flavor than onions and are suited to dishes that are cooked quickly. Both the white and green parts are used.

Seaweed (31) Dried seaweed is widely used in Japanese cooking to impart a salty, rich flavor of the sea. Nori is a dried, flat seaweed used for making sushi. Kelp is also dried and should be soaked in water before use.

Sesame seeds (32) White sesame seeds are widely used in Japanese cooking. The seeds should be dry-fried, to release their flavor. Toasted seeds

are often ground finely to thicken and enrich sauces.

Shiitaki mushrooms (33) Fresh shiitaki mushrooms have a rich, meaty flavor that combines especially well with shellfish and poultry. Shiitake are widely available dried and yield a good flavor when soaked in boiling water.

Sichuan pepper (34) Sichuan pepper has a warm, fruity flavor without the intense heat of white or black peppercorns. To obtain the best flavor, Sichuan pepper should be dry-fried and coarsely ground before use.

Somen noodles (35) Somen noodles are made from wheat flour and are an important part of the Japanese diet. It is most common to find somen noodles in a flavorsome chicken broth.

Star anise (37) This attractive spice is sold in star-shaped pods and carries the soft scent of aniseed. The pods are used whole or ground to flavor sweet and savory dishes.

Star fruit (38) Star fruit have a sweet scented flavor when ripe and can be eaten cooked or raw in fruit salads.

Sweet potato (39) The sweet richness of this red tuber marries well with the hot and sour flavors of Southeast Asia. In Japan, the sweet potato is used to make delicious candies.

Tomatoes (40) Both ripe and under-ripe tomatoes feature in the cooking of Southeast Asia. Under-ripe fruit are used in slow-cooking meat dishes and lend a special sour taste.

HOT CHILI DUCK WITH CRABMEAT AND CASHEW NUT SAUCE

Bhed Sune Khan

This dish may be served with Thai rice and a dish of Thai Dipping Sauce.

SERVES 4–6

Ingredients
6lb duck
5 cups water, to cover
2 lime leaves
1 tsp salt
2–3 small red chilies, seeded and finely chopped

5 tsp sugar
½ tsp salt
2 tbsp coriander seeds
1 tsp caraway seeds
4oz raw cashew nuts, chopped
1 piece lemon grass, 3in long, shredded
1 piece galingal or fresh ginger, 1in long, peeled and finely chopped
2 cloves garlic, crushed

4 shallots, or 1 medium onion, finely chopped
1 piece shrimp paste, ¾in square
1oz cilantro, white root or stem, finely chopped
6oz frozen white crabmeat, thawed
2oz unsweetened cream of coconut
1 small bunch cilantro, chopped, to garnish

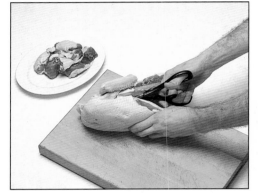

1 To portion the duck into manageable pieces, first remove the legs. Separate the thighs from the drumsticks and chop each thigh and drumstick into 2 pieces. Trim away the lower half of the duck with kitchen scissors. Cut the breast piece in half down the middle, then chop each half into 4 pieces.

2 Put the duck flesh and bones into a large saucepan and cover with the water. Add the lime leaves and salt, bring to a boil and simmer, uncovered, for 35–40 minutes, until the meat is tender. Discard the duck bones, skim off the fat from the stock, and set aside.

3 To make the curry sauce, grind the red chilies together with the sugar and salt using a pestle and mortar or a food processor. Dry-fry the coriander and caraway seeds and the cashew nuts in a wok to release their flavor, about 1–2 minutes. Add the chilies, the lemon grass, galingal or ginger, garlic, and shallots or onion, and reduce to a smooth paste. Add the shrimp paste and cilantro.

4 Add 1 cup of the liquid in which the duck was cooked and blend until a thin paste is obtained.

5 Stir the curry seasoning in with the duck, bring to a boil, and simmer, uncovered, for 20–25 minutes.

6 Add the crabmeat and cream of coconut and simmer briefly. Turn out onto an attractive serving dish, decorate with cilantro and serve.

DRY BEEF CURRY WITH PEANUT AND LIME

Nua Pad Prik

Dry curries originated from the mountainous northern regions of Thailand but are popular throughout the country. This dry beef curry is usually served with a moist dish such as Ragout of Shellfish with Sweet Scented Basil, or Thai Chicken and Shrimp Soup. The curry is equally delicious made with a lean leg or shoulder of lamb.

SERVES 4–6

Ingredients
2lb stewing beef, (chuck is best), finely chopped
14oz canned coconut milk
1¼ cups beef stock

Red curry paste
2 tbsp coriander seeds
1 tsp cumin seeds
6 green cardamom pods, seeds only
½ tsp ground nutmeg
¼ tsp ground clove
½ tsp ground cinnamon
4 tsp paprika
zest of 1 mandarin orange, finely chopped
4–5 small red chilies, seeded and finely chopped
5 tsp sugar
½ tsp salt
1 piece lemon grass, 4in long, shredded
3 cloves garlic, crushed
1 piece galingal or fresh ginger, ¾in long, peeled and finely chopped
4 red shallots or 1 medium red onion, finely chopped
1 piece shrimp paste, ¾in square
2oz cilantro, white root or stem, chopped
juice of 2½ limes
2 tbsp vegetable oil
2 tbsp chunky peanut butter
1 lime, sliced, to garnish
1 large red chili, sliced, to garnish
1 small bunch cilantro, shredded, to garnish

1 Place the meat in the freezer for 30–40 minutes until firm. Slice the meat thinly, cut into strips, and chop finely. Strain the coconut milk into a bowl.

2 Place the thin part and half of the thick part of the milk in a large saucepan. Add the beef, and beef stock, bring to a boil, cover, and simmer for 50 minutes.

3 To make the curry paste, dry-fry the coriander, cumin seeds, and cardamom in a wok for 1–2 minutes. Combine with the nutmeg, clove, cinnamon, paprika, and the zest of the mandarin orange. Pound the chilies with the sugar and salt. Add the chili paste, lemon grass, garlic, galingal or ginger, shallots or onion, and shrimp paste. Lastly add the cilantro, juice of ½ lime, and oil.

4 Place a cupful of the cooking liquid in a wok, and add 2–3 tbsp of the curry paste according to taste. Boil rapidly until the liquid has reduced completely. Add the remainder of the coconut milk, the peanut butter, and the beef. Simmer, uncovered, for 15–20 minutes. Stir in the remaining lime juice. Serve decorated with the lime, chili and cilantro.

GREEN CURRY-COCONUT CHICKEN

Kaeng Khieu Wan Gai

The recipe given here for green curry paste is a complex one and therefore takes time to make properly. Pork, shrimp and fish can all be used instead of chicken, but cooking times must be adjusted accordingly.

SERVES 4–6

Ingredients
2½lb chicken, without giblets
2½ cups canned coconut milk
1½ cups chicken stock
2 lime leaves

Green curry paste
2 tsp coriander seeds

½ tsp caraway or cumin seeds
3–4 medium green chilies, finely chopped
4 tsp sugar
2 tsp salt
1 piece lemon grass, 3in long
1 piece galingal or fresh ginger, ¾in long, peeled and finely chopped
3 cloves garlic, crushed
4 shallots or 1 medium onion, finely chopped
1 piece shrimp paste, ¾in square

3 tbsp cilantro leaves, finely chopped
3 tbsp fresh mint or basil, finely chopped
½ tsp nutmeg powder
2 tbsp vegetable oil
12oz sweet potatoes, peeled and roughly chopped
12oz winter squash, peeled, seeded, and roughly chopped
4oz French green beans, topped, tailed and halved
1 small bunch cilantro, shredded, to garnish

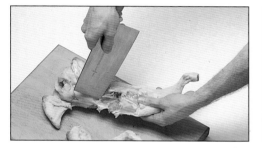

1 To prepare the chicken, remove the legs, then separate the thighs from the drumsticks. Separate the lower part of the chicken carcass by cutting through the rib section with kitchen scissors. Divide the breast part in half down the middle, then chop each half in two. Remove skin from all pieces and set aside.

2 Strain the coconut milk into a bowl, reserving the thick part. Place the chicken in a stainless steel or enamel saucepan, cover with the thin part of the coconut milk and the stock. Add the lime leaves, and simmer, uncovered, for 40 minutes. Remove the chicken from the bone and set aside.

3 Dry-fry the coriander and caraway or cumin seeds. Grind the chilies with the sugar and salt to make a smooth paste. Combine the seeds from the wok with the chilies, the lemon grass, galingal or ginger, garlic, and shallots, then grind smoothly. Add the next 5 ingredients.

4 Place a cupful of the cooking liquid in a large wok. Add 4–5 tbsp of the curry paste to the liquid according to taste. Boil rapidly until the liquid has reduced completely. Add the chicken stock, chicken meat, sweet potatoes, squash, and beans. Simmer for 10–15 minutes until the potatoes are cooked. Just before serving, stir in the thick part of the coconut milk and simmer until thick. Serve decorated with the shredded cilantro.

THAI STEAMED FISH WITH A CITRUS MARINADE

Pla Chien

Serve Thai rice or fine rice noodles as an accompaniment to this dish.

SERVES 4–6

Ingredients
3lb parrot fish, pomfret, plaice, or sea bream, gutted with heads on
2 small red chilies, seeded and finely chopped
1 tbsp sugar
2 cloves garlic, crushed
3 scallions, white part only, chopped
1 piece fresh galingal or fresh ginger, 1in long, peeled and finely chopped
juice of 1 mandarin orange
zest of 1 mandarin orange, finely chopped
1 tbsp tamarind sauce
1 tbsp fish sauce
2 tbsp light soy sauce
juice of 1 lime
1 tbsp vegetable oil
2 limes, quartered, to garnish
4 scallion curls, to garnish

1 Wash the fish thoroughly and score 3–4 times with a sharp knife on each side to allow the marinade to penetrate deeply. Place the fish in a shallow dish that will fit in the base of a steamer. You can also wrap the fish loosely in foil.

2 Grind the chili and sugar together using a pestle and mortar or food processor, add the garlic, scallion, galingal or ginger, and the zest of the mandarin orange. Combine well. Lastly add the tamarind, fish and soy sauces, the lime juice, and vegetable oil, then spread evenly over the fish. Leave to marinate for at least 1 hour.

3 Cook the fish in a covered steamer for 25–30 minutes. Lift the fish onto a serving plate and decorate with wedges of lime and the scallion curls.

PORK AND PEANUT PICK-ME-UPS

Ma Hor

With a Thai meal, it is not customary to have a starter. Instead, appetizers are served with drinks beforehand.

MAKES 12

Ingredients
1 tbsp vegetable oil
2 shallots, or 1 small onion, finely chopped
1 clove garlic, crushed
1 piece fresh ginger, ¾in long, peeled and finely chopped

1 small red chili, seeded and finely chopped
5oz ground pork, or 5oz fresh pork sausage meat
2 tbsp peanut butter
1 tbsp fish sauce
juice of ½ lime
4 tsp sugar
2 tbsp chopped cilantro leaves
4 clementines, peeled and thickly sliced

6 ramboutans, or lychees, peeled and pitted
1 small pineapple, peeled, cored, and sliced
1 firm pear, peeled, cored, and sliced
1 lime, cut into small wedges, to garnish
12 cilantro leaves, to garnish

1 Heat the oil and fry the next 4 ingredients. Add the pork and cook for 10 minutes.

2 Add the peanut butter, fish sauce, lime juice, sugar, and chopped cilantro.

3 Spoon the topping onto pieces of fruit. Decorate with lime and cilantro leaves.

THAI DIPPING SAUCE

Nam Prik

Nam Prik is the most common dipping sauce in Thailand. It has a fiery strength, so use with caution.

MAKES ½ CUP

Ingredients
1 tbsp vegetable oil
1 piece shrimp paste, ½in square, or
  1 tbsp fish sauce
2 cloves garlic, finely sliced
1 piece fresh ginger, ¾in long, peeled and finely
  chopped
3 small red chilies, seeded and chopped
1 tbsp finely chopped cilantro root or stem
4 tsp sugar
3 tbsp dark soy sauce
juice of ½ lime

1 Heat the vegetable oil in a wok, add the shrimp paste or fish sauce, garlic, ginger, and chilies and soften without coloring, for about 1–2 minutes.

2 Remove from the heat and add the cilantro, sugar, soy sauce, and lime juice. Nam Prik Sauce will keep in an airtight container for up to 10 days.

HOT COCONUT SHRIMP AND PAW PAW SALAD

Yam Ma-La-Kaw Prik

This dish may be served as an accompaniment to beef and chicken dishes.

SERVES 4–6

Ingredients
8oz fresh or cooked shrimp tails, peeled and
  deveined
2 ripe paw paws, or papayas
8oz lettuce leaves, Napa cabbage and young
  spinach

1 firm tomato, skinned, seeded, and roughly
  chopped
3 scallions, shredded

Dressing
3 tbsp unsweetened cream of coconut
6 tbsp vegetable oil
juice of 1 lime

½ tsp hot chili sauce
2 tsp fish sauce (optional)
1 tsp sugar
1 small bunch cilantro, shredded, to garnish
1 large chili, sliced, to garnish

1 To make the dressing, place the cream of coconut in a screw-top jar and add the vegetable oil, lime juice, chili sauce, fish sauce if using, and sugar. Shake well and set aside. Do not refrigerate.

2 If using fresh shrimp tails, cover with cold water in a saucepan, bring to a boil, and simmer for no longer than 2 minutes. Drain and set aside.

3 To prepare the paw paws or papayas, cut each in half from top to bottom and remove the black seeds with a spoon. Peel away the outer skin and cut the flesh into even-sized pieces. Wash the salad leaves and toss in a bowl. Add the other ingredients. Pour on the dressing and serve.

Red Curry Beef with Tamarind

Kang Mussaman Nuea

This red curry can also be made using diced lamb, in which case reduce the cooking time by 30 minutes.

SERVES 4–6

Ingredients
2lb stewing beef (chuck is best)
14oz canned coconut milk
1¼ cups beef stock

Red curry paste
2 tbsp coriander seeds
1 tsp cumin seeds
6 green cardamom pods, seeds only
½ tsp ground nutmeg
¼ tsp ground cloves
½ tsp ground cinnamon

4 tsp paprika
zest of 1 mandarin orange, finely chopped
4–5 small red chilies, seeded and finely chopped
5 tsp sugar
½ tsp salt
1 piece lemon grass, 4in long, shredded
3 cloves garlic, crushed
1 piece galingal or fresh ginger, ¾in long, peeled and finely chopped
4 red shallots or 1 medium red onion, finely chopped
1 piece shrimp paste, ¾in square
2oz cilantro, white root or stem, chopped
2 tbsp vegetable oil

12oz new potatoes, peeled and roughly chopped
12oz pumpkin or winter squash
7oz canned bamboo shoots, sliced
2 tbsp smooth peanut butter
2 tbsp tamarind sauce
juice of 2 limes
1 small bunch cilantro, to garnish

1 Cut the beef into 1in dice and place in a stainless steel saucepan.

2 Place the coconut milk in a fine strainer and allow the liquid to drain into a bowl. Add all of the liquid and half of the coconut milk solids to the saucepan. Add the stock, bring to a boil, and simmer, uncovered, for 1 hour. Strain and set aside.

3 Dry-fry the coriander, cumin seeds, and cardamom in a wok for 1–2 minutes. Combine with the nutmeg, clove, cinnamon, paprika and mandarin zest, and grind. Pound the chilies with the sugar and salt. Add the chili paste, lemon grass, garlic, galingal, shallots, and shrimp paste. Add the cilantro and oil and reduce.

4 Place a cupful of the cooking liquid in a large wok. Add 2–3 tbsp of the paste. Boil rapidly to reduce the liquid. Add the peanut butter and tamarind sauce. Add the beef, potatoes, pumpkin, and bamboo shoots and simmer for 20–25 minutes until the potatoes are cooked. Stir in the coconut milk solids and the lime juice. Return to a gentle simmer. Decorate, and serve with Thai rice.

COCONUT MILK

Coconut milk is used to enrich and flavor many dishes in the Far East. Only the Japanese choose not to include it in their cooking. Coconut milk is not, as many suppose, the liquid found inside the nut. Although this thin liquid does make a refreshing drink, the coconut milk used for cooking is processed from the white flesh of the nut. If left to stand, the thick part of the milk will rise to the surface like cream. If the milk is cold the thick part of the milk will separate more easily. Choose a coconut with plenty of milk inside. Shake the nut firmly. If you cannot hear the milk sloshing around, the flesh will be difficult to remove. If you can find a coconut with its green husk and fibre attached, the flesh will almost certainly be soft and creamy white. Fresh coconut milk will keep in a cool place for up to 10 days. If kept in the refrigerator, allow to soften at room temperature before using.

MAKES 1¾ cups

Ingredients
2 fresh coconuts
5 cups water, just boiled

1 Hold the coconut over a bowl to collect the liquid. With the back of a large knife or cleaver, crack open the coconut by striking it cleanly.

2 Scrape out the white meat with a citrus zester or a rounded butter curler. Place the coconut meat in a food processor with half of the water.

3 Process for 1 minute, then pass through a food mill fitted with a fine disk, catching the milk in a bowl beneath. Alternatively, squeeze the coconut meat with your hands and press through a nylon strainer. Return the coconut meat to the mill or food processor with the remainder of the water, blend, and press for a second time. Allow the milk to settle for 30 minutes (creamy solids will rise to the surface). Sometimes the solids should be poured off and added later as a thickener.

Cook's tip

Coconut milk can be obtained directly from coconut flesh – this gives the creamiest milk. It is also available in a can, as a soluble powder, and in block form. Coconut milk which is pre-packaged in this way makes a useful addition to sauces and dressings.

RAGOUT OF SHELLFISH WITH SWEET SCENTED BASIL

Po-Tak

Green curry paste can be used to accompany other dishes, such as Green Curry-Coconut Chicken. Curry pastes will keep for up to 3 weeks in the refrigerator if stored in an airtight container.

SERVES 4–6

Ingredients
2½ cups fresh mussels in their shells, cleaned
8oz medium cuttle fish or squid
12oz monkfish, hokey, or red snapper, skinned
5oz fresh or cooked shrimp tails, peeled and deveined
4 scallops, sliced (optional)
14oz canned coconut milk
1¼ cups chicken or vegetable stock
3oz green beans, trimmed and cooked
2oz canned bamboo shoots, drained
1 ripe tomato, skinned, seeded, and roughly chopped

Green curry paste
2 tsp coriander seeds
½ tsp caraway or cumin seeds
3–4 medium green chilies, finely chopped
4 tsp sugar
2 tsp salt
1 piece lemon grass, 3in long
1 piece galingal or fresh ginger, ¾in long, peeled and finely chopped
3 cloves garlic, crushed
4 shallots or 1 medium onion, finely chopped
1 piece shrimp paste, ¾in square
2oz cilantro leaves, finely chopped
3 tbsp fresh mint or basil, finely chopped
½ tsp ground nutmeg

2 tbsp vegetable oil
4 sprigs large-leaf basil, torn, to garnish

1 Place the mussels in a stainless steel or enamel saucepan, add 4 tbsp of water, cover, steam open and cook for 6–8 minutes. Take ¾ of the mussels out of their shells (discard any which don't open), strain the cooking liquid, and set aside.

2 To prepare the cuttle fish or squid, trim off the tentacles beneath the eye. Rinse under cold running water, discarding the gut. Remove the cuttle shell from inside the body and rub off the paper-thin skin. Cut the body open and score, criss-cross, with a sharp knife. Cut into strips and set aside.

3 To make the green curry paste, dry-fry the coriander and caraway or cumin seeds in a wok to release their flavour. Grind the chilies with the sugar and salt using a pestle and mortar or food processor to make a smooth paste. Combine the seeds from the wok with the chilies, add the lemon grass, galingal or ginger, garlic, and shallots or onion, then grind smoothly. Add the shrimp paste, cilantro, mint or basil, nutmeg, and vegetable oil. Combine well. There may seem to be a lot of cilantro and mint at this stage, but their volume will reduce considerably when ground with the other spices.

4 Pour the coconut milk into a strainer. Pour the thin part of the milk together with the chicken or vegetable stock into a wok. The coconut milk solids are added later. Add 4–5 tbsp of the green curry paste according to taste. You can add more paste later if you need to. Boil rapidly until the liquid has reduced completely.

5 Add the coconut milk solids, then add the cuttle fish or squid and monkfish, hokey or red snapper. Simmer, uncovered, for 15–20 minutes. Then add the shrimp, scallops, and cooked mussels with the beans, bamboo shoots, and tomato. Simmer for 2–3 minutes, transfer to a bowl, and decorate with the basil and chilies.

Thai Fruit and Vegetable Salad

Yam Chomphu

This fruit salad is presented with the main course and serves as a cooler to counteract the heat of the chilies.

SERVES 4–6

Ingredients
1 small pineapple
1 small mango, peeled and sliced
1 green apple, cored and sliced
6 ramboutans or lychees, peeled and pitted
4oz green beans, trimmed, and halved
1 medium red onion, sliced
1 small cucumber, cut into short fingers
4oz bean sprouts
2 scallions, sliced

1 ripe tomato, quartered
8oz romaine, bib, or iceberg lettuce leaves

Coconut dipping sauce
5 tbsp unsweetened cream of coconut
2 tbsp sugar
¼ tsp chili sauce
1 tbsp fish sauce
juice of 1 lime

Cook's tip

Creamed coconut is sold in 7oz blocks and may be found in specialist food stores. In warm weather, creamed coconut should be stored in a cool place to keep it from softening. To use, soften with boiling water to achieve a creamy consistency. Canned cream of coconut can also be used, but make sure you buy the unsweetened variety.

1 To make the coconut dipping sauce, measure the coconut, sugar, and boiling water into a screw-top jar. Add the chili and fish sauces and lime juice and shake.

2 Trim both ends of the pineapple with a serrated knife, then cut away the outer skin. Remove the central core with an apple corer. Alternatively, cut the pineapple into 4 down the middle and remove the core with a knife. Roughly chop the pineapple and set aside with the other fruits.

3 Bring a small saucepan of salted water to the boil and cook the beans for 3–4 minutes. Refresh under cold running water and set aside. To serve, arrange the fruits and vegetables into small heaps in a shallow bowl. Serve the coconut sauce separately as a dip.

Sweet Cucumber Cooler

Ajad

Sweet dipping sauces such as this bring instant relief to the hot chili flavors of Thai food.

MAKES ½ CUP

Ingredients
5 tbsp water
2 tbsp sugar
½ tsp salt
1 tbsp rice or white wine vinegar
¼ small cucumber, quartered and thinly sliced
2 shallots, or 1 small red onion, thinly sliced

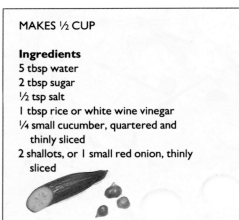

1 Measure the water, sugar, salt, and vinegar into a stainless steel or enamel saucepan. Bring to a boil and simmer until the sugar has dissolved, not more than 1 minute.

2 Allow to cool. Add the cucumber and shallots or onion and serve at room temperature.

HOT CHILI CHICKEN WITH GINGER AND LEMON-GRASS

Ga Xao Xa Ot

This dish can also be prepared using duck legs. Be sure to remove the jointed parts of the drumsticks and thigh bones to make the meat easier to eat with chopsticks.

SERVES 4–6

Ingredients
3 chicken legs (thighs and drumsticks)
1 tbsp vegetable oil
1 piece fresh ginger, ¾in long, peeled and finely chopped

1 clove garlic, crushed
1 small red chili, seeded and finely chopped
1 piece lemon grass, 2in long, shredded
⅔ cup chicken stock
1 tbsp fish sauce (optional)
2 tsp sugar
½ tsp salt

juice of ½ lemon
2oz raw peanuts
2 scallions, shredded
1 zest of mandarin orange or satsuma, shredded
2 tbsp chopped mint
rice or rice noodles, to serve

1 With the heel of the knife, chop through the narrow end of the drumsticks. Remove the jointed parts of the drumsticks and thigh bones, then remove the skin.

2 Heat the oil in a large wok or frying pan. Add the chicken, ginger, garlic, chili and lemongrass and cook for 3–4 minutes. Add the chicken stock, fish sauce if using, sugar, salt, and lemon juice. Cover and simmer gently for 30–35 minutes.

3 To prepare the peanuts for the topping, the red skin must be removed. To do this, broil or roast the peanuts under a steady heat until evenly brown, for about 2–3 minutes. Transfer the nuts to a clean cloth and rub briskly to loosen the skins.

4 Serve the chicken scattered with roasted peanuts, shredded scallions, and the zest of the mandarin orange or satsuma. Serve with rice or rice noodles.

CRAB, PORK, AND MUSHROOM SPRING ROLLS

Cha Gio

If you cannot obtain ground pork, use the meat from the equivalent weight of best-quality pork sausages. Filled spring rolls can be made in advance and kept in the refrigerator ready for frying.

MAKES 12 ROLLS

Ingredients
1oz rice noodles
2oz Chinese mushrooms (shiitake), fresh or dried
1 tbsp vegetable oil
4 scallions, chopped
1 small carrot, grated
6oz ground pork
4oz white crabmeat
1 tsp fish sauce (optional)
salt and pepper
12 frozen spring roll skins, defrosted
2 tbsp cornstarch paste
vegetable oil, for deep-frying
1 head iceberg or bibb lettuce, to serve
1 bunch mint or basil, to serve
1 bunch cilantro leaves, to serve
½ hothouse cucumber, sliced, to serve

1 Bring a large saucepan of salted water to the boil, and simmer the noodles for 8 minutes. Cut the noodles into finger-length pieces. If the mushrooms are dried, soak them in boiling water for about 10 minutes before slicing thinly.

2 To make the filling, heat the oil in a wok or frying pan, add the scallions, carrot, and pork and cook for 8–10 minutes. Remove from the heat, then add the crabmeat, fish sauce, and seasoning. Add the noodles and mushrooms, and set aside.

3 To fill the rolls, brush one spring roll skin at a time with the cornstarch paste, then place 1 tsp of the filling onto the skin. Fold the edges towards the middle and roll evenly to make a neat cigar shape. The paste will help seal the wrapper.

4 Heat the oil in a wok or deep-fryer until hot. Fry the spring rolls two at a time in the oil for 6–8 minutes. Make sure the fat is not too hot or the mixture inside will not heat through properly. Serve on a bed of salad leaves, mint, cilantro, and cucumber.

HOT AND SOUR CHICKEN SALAD

Ga Nuong Ngu Vi

This salad is also delicious with shrimp. Allow 1lb of fresh shrimp tails to serve 4.

SERVES 4–6	1 clove garlic, crushed	2 tsp fish sauce (optional)
	1 tbsp crunchy peanut butter	4oz bean sprouts
Ingredients	2 tbsp chopped cilantro leaves	1 head Napa cabbage, roughly shredded
2 skinless chicken breasts	1 tsp sugar	2 medium carrots, cut into thin sticks
1 small red chili, seeded and finely chopped	½ tsp salt	1 red onion, cut into fine rings
1 piece fresh ginger, ½in long, peeled and finely chopped	1 tbsp rice or white wine vinegar	2 large pickles, sliced
	4 tbsp vegetable oil	

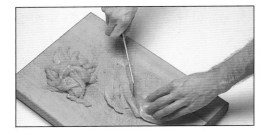  

1 Slice the chicken thinly, place in a shallow bowl and set aside. Grind the chili, ginger, and garlic in a pestle and mortar. Add the peanut butter, cilantro, sugar, and salt.

2 Then add the vinegar, 2 tbsp of the oil and the fish sauce if using. Combine well. Cover the chicken with the spice mixture and leave to marinate for at least 2–3 hours.

3 Heat the remaining 2 tbsp of oil in a wok or frying pan. Add the chicken and cook for 10–12 minutes, tossing the meat occasionally. Serve arranged on the salad.

ALFALFA-CRAB SALAD WITH CRISPY FRIED NOODLES

Goi Gia

Alfalfa sprouts are available in many supermarkets. Alternatively, you can grow your own sprouts from seeds.

SERVES 4–6	1 small iceberg or bibb lettuce	½ small red chili, seeded and finely chopped
	4 sprigs cilantro, roughly chopped	1 piece stem ginger in syrup, cut into matchsticks
Ingredients	1 ripe tomato, skinned, seeded and diced	2 tsp stem ginger syrup
vegetable oil, for deep-frying	4 sprigs fresh mint, roughly chopped	2 tsp soy sauce
2oz Chinese rice noodles, uncooked		juice of ½ lime
2 dressed crabs, or 5oz frozen white crabmeat, thawed	**Sesame lime dressing**	
4oz alfalfa sprouts	3 tbsp vegetable oil	
	1 tsp sesame oil	

1 Combine the vegetable and sesame oils in a bowl. Add the chili, stem ginger, stem ginger syrup, soy sauce and the lime juice.

2 Heat the oil in a deep-fryer to 385°F. Fry the noodles, one handful at a time, until crisp. Lift out and dry on paper.

3 Flake the white crabmeat into a bowl and toss with the alfalfa sprouts. Serve on a nest of noodles and tossed salad ingredients.

PORK BALLS WITH A MINTED PEANUT SAUCE

Nem Nuong

This recipe is equally delicious made with chicken breasts.

SERVES 4–6

Ingredients
10oz leg of pork, trimmed and diced
1 piece fresh ginger, ½in long,
 peeled and grated
1 clove garlic, crushed
2 tsp sesame oil
1 tbsp medium-dry sherry
1 tbsp soy sauce
1 tsp sugar

1 egg white
½ tsp salt
a pinch of white pepper
12oz long-grain rice, washed and
 cooked for 15 minutes
2oz ham, thickly sliced and diced
1 iceberg or bibb lettuce, to serve

Minted peanut sauce
2 tbsp smooth peanut butter
juice of 1 lime
1 red chili, seeded and finely chopped
1 clove garlic, crushed
1 tbsp freshly chopped mint
1 tbsp freshly chopped cilantro
⅓ cup unsweetened cream of coconut
1 tbsp fish sauce (optional)

1 To make the pork balls, place the diced pork, ginger, and garlic in a food processor and blend until smooth, about 2–3 minutes. Add the sesame oil, sherry, soy sauce, and sugar and blend. Add the egg white.

2 Spread the cooked rice and ham on a shallow dish. Using wet hands, shape the pork mixture into thumb-sized balls. Roll in the rice to cover and pierce each ball with a bamboo skewer.

3 To make the sauce, place the peanut butter in a bowl with the lime juice, chili, garlic, mint, and cilantro. Combine evenly, then add the cream of coconut and season with the fish sauce if using.

4 Place the pork balls in a bamboo steamer, cover, and steam over a saucepan of boiling water for 8–10 minutes. Arrange all the lettuce leaves on a large serving plate. Place the pork balls on the leaves with the dipping sauce on the side.

EXOTIC FRUIT SALAD

Hoa Qua Tron

A variety of fruits can be used for this salad depending on what is available. Look out for mandarin oranges, star fruit, paw paw, kiwi fruit, and passion fruit.

SERVES 4–6

Ingredients
6 tbsp sugar
1¼ cups water
2 tbsp stem ginger syrup
2 pieces star anise
1 piece cinnamon stick, 1 in long
1 clove
juice of ½ lemon
2 sprigs mint

1 medium pineapple
1 mango, peeled and sliced
2 bananas, sliced
8 lychees, fresh or canned
8oz fresh strawberries, trimmed and halved
2 pieces stem ginger, cut into sticks

1 Measure the sugar into a saucepan, and add the water, ginger syrup, spices, lemon juice, and mint. Bring to a boil and simmer for 3 minutes. Strain into a large bowl and allow to cool.

2 Remove both the top and bottom from the mango and remove the outer skin. Stand the mango on one end and remove the flesh in two pieces either side of the flat pit. Slice evenly and add to the syrup. Add the bananas, lychees, strawberries, and ginger. Chill until ready to serve.

3 Cut the pineapple in half down the centre. Loosen the flesh with a small serrated knife and remove to form two boat shapes. Cut the flesh into large chunks and place in the cooled syrup.

4 Spoon the fruit salad into the pineapple halves and bring to the table on a large serving dish. There will be enough fruit salad left over to refill the pineapple halves.

PORK AND NOODLE BROTH WITH SHRIMP

Pho

This quick and delicious recipe can be made with 7oz boneless chicken breast instead of pork tenderloin.

SERVES 4–6

Ingredients
12oz pork chops or 7oz pork tenderloin
8oz fresh shrimp tails or cooked shrimp
5oz thin egg noodles
1 tbsp vegetable oil
2 tsp sesame oil
4 shallots, or 1 medium onion, sliced
1 tbsp fresh ginger, finely sliced
1 clove garlic, crushed

1 tsp granulated sugar
6¼ cups chicken stock
2 lime leaves
3 tbsp fish sauce
juice of ½ lime
4 sprigs cilantro leaves, to garnish
chopped green part of 2 scallions, to garnish

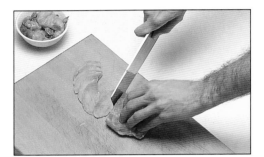

1 If using pork chops, trim away fat and bone completely. Place the meat in the freezer for 30 minutes to firm but not freeze the meat. Slice the meat thinly and set aside. Peel and devein the shrimp, if fresh.

2 Bring a large saucepan of salted water to the boil and simmer the noodles for the time stated on the packet. Drain and refresh under cold running water. Set aside.

3 Heat the vegetable and sesame oils in a large saucepan, add the shallots, and brown evenly, for 3–4 minutes. Remove from the pan and set aside.

4 Add the ginger, garlic, sugar, and chicken stock and bring to a simmer with the lime leaves. Add the fish sauce and lime juice. Add the pork, then simmer for 15 minutes. Add the shrimp and noodles and simmer for 3–4 minutes. Serve in shallow soup bowls and decorate with the cilantro leaves, the green part of the scallions and the browned shallots.

VIETNAMESE DIPPING SAUCE

Nuoc Cham

Serve this dip in a small bowl as an accompaniment to spring rolls or meat dishes.

MAKES ⅔ CUP

Ingredients
1–2 small red chilies, seeded and finely chopped
1 clove garlic, crushed
1 tbsp roasted peanuts
4 tbsp coconut milk
2 tbsp fish sauce
juice of 1 lime
2 tsp sugar
1 tsp chopped cilantro leaves

1 Crush the red chili together with the garlic and peanuts using a pestle and mortar or food processor.

2 Add the coconut milk, fish sauce, lime juice, sugar, and cilantro.

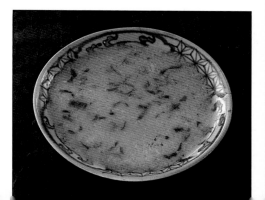

HANDLING CHILIES

Chilies are an important part of Eastern cookery and should be handled with care. The pungent oils released when chilies are cut can be harmful to sensitive parts of the skin, especially to eyes and lips. Be sure to wash your hands thoroughly with soap and water after touching cut chilies.

1 The severe heat of red and green chilies is contained in the seeds. Unless you like fiercely hot food, the seeds should be discarded before using. It is most practical to wash the seeds away under cold running water.

2 A useful chili flavoring can be made by storing chilies in a jar of oil. Allow the hot flavors to merge for 3 weeks before using. Chili oil is used to add a gentle heat to many Eastern dishes.

CUCUMBER AND CARROT GARNISHES

Presentation is an important part of Southeast Asian cooking. These vegetable decorations are easily prepared.

MAKES 2 DECORATIVE GARNISHES

Ingredients
½ hothouse cucumber
1 large carrot

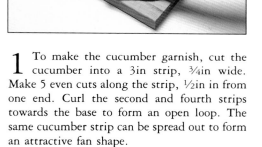

1 To make the cucumber garnish, cut the cucumber into a 3in strip, ¾in wide. Make 5 even cuts along the strip, ½in in from one end. Curl the second and fourth strips towards the base to form an open loop. The same cucumber strip can be spread out to form an attractive fan shape.

2 To make the carrot garnish, peel the carrot and cut into ¼in slices lengthways. Trim the slices into rectangles, ¾in × 3in. Make a ¼in cut along one edge of the carrot so that the strip is still joined. Make a second cut in the other direction, again so that the strip is joined. Bend the two ends together so that they cross over. This garnish can also be fashioned with giant white radish, cucumber, and lemon peel.

MAIN COURSE SPICY SHRIMP AND NOODLE SOUP

Laksa Lemak

This dish is served as a hot coconut broth with a separate platter of shrimp, fish, and noodles. Diners are invited to add their own choice of accompaniment to the broth.

SERVES 4–6

Ingredients

1oz raw cashew nuts
3 shallots, or 1 medium onion, sliced
1 piece lemongrass, 2in long, shredded
2 cloves garlic, crushed
2 tbsp vegetable oil
1 piece shrimp paste, ½in square, or
   1 tbsp fish sauce
1 tbsp mild curry paste
14oz canned coconut milk

½ chicken stock cube
3 curry leaves (optional)
1lb white fish fillet, cod, haddock, or whiting
8oz shrimp tails, fresh or cooked
1 small romaine lettuce, shredded
4oz bean sprouts
3 scallions, shredded
½ hothouse cucumber, sliced and shredded
5oz Laksa noodles (spaghetti-size rice noodles),
   soaked for 10 minutes before cooking
Shrimp Crackers, to serve

Cook's tip

To serve, line a large serving platter with the shredded lettuce leaves. Arrange the salad ingredients in neat piles together with the cooked fish, shrimp, and noodles. Serve the salad with a bowl of Shrimp Crackers and the broth in a lidded stoneware pot.

1 Grind the cashew nuts using a pestle and mortar or food processor with the shallots or onion, lemongrass and garlic. Cook the noodles according to the instructions.

2 Heat the oil in a large wok or saucepan, add the contents of the mortar or food processor, and fry until the nuts begin to brown, for about 1–2 minutes.

3 Add the shrimp paste or fish sauce and curry paste, followed by the coconut milk, stock cube, and curry leaves. Simmer for 10 minutes.

4 Cut the white fish into bite-size pieces. Place the fish and shrimp in a large frying basket, immerse into the simmering coconut stock, and cook for 3–4 minutes.

SESAME BAKED FISH WITH A HOT GINGER MARINADE

Panggang Bungkus

Tropical fish are found increasingly in supermarkets, but Asian markets usually have a wider selection.

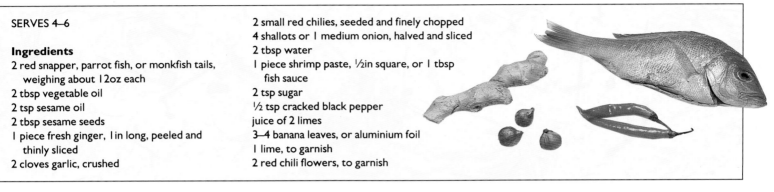

SERVES 4–6

Ingredients

2 red snapper, parrot fish, or monkfish tails, weighing about 12oz each
2 tbsp vegetable oil
2 tsp sesame oil
2 tbsp sesame seeds
1 piece fresh ginger, 1in long, peeled and thinly sliced
2 cloves garlic, crushed

2 small red chilies, seeded and finely chopped
4 shallots or 1 medium onion, halved and sliced
2 tbsp water
1 piece shrimp paste, ½in square, or 1 tbsp fish sauce
2 tsp sugar
½ tsp cracked black pepper
juice of 2 limes
3–4 banana leaves, or aluminium foil
1 lime, to garnish
2 red chili flowers, to garnish

1 Clean the fish inside and out under cold running water. Pat dry with paper towels. Score both sides of each fish deeply with a knife to enable the marinade to penetrate effectively. If using parrot fish, rub with fine salt and leave to stand for 15 minutes. (This will remove the chalky coral flavor often associated with the parrot fish.)

2 To make the marinade, heat the vegetable and sesame oils in a wok, add the sesame seeds and fry until golden. Add the ginger, garlic, chilies and shallots or onion and soften over a gentle heat without burning. Add the water, shrimp paste or fish sauce, sugar, pepper, and lime juice, simmer for 2–3 minutes and allow to cool.

3 If using banana leaves, remove the central stem and discard. Soften the leaves by dipping in boiling water. To keep them supple, rub all over with vegetable oil. Spread the marinade over the fish, wrap in the banana leaf, and fasten with a bamboo skewer, or wrap the fish in foil. Leave the fish in a cool place to allow the flavors to mingle, for up to 3 hours.

4 Preheat the oven to 350°F or light a barbecue and allow the embers to settle to a steady glow. Place the wrapped fish on a wire rack or baking sheet and cook for between 35–40 minutes.

SPICY CLAY-POT CHICKEN

Ayam Golek

Clay-pot cooking stems from the practice of burying a glazed pot in the embers of an open fire. The gentle heat surrounds the base and keeps the liquid inside at a slow simmer, similar to the modern-day pot roast.

SERVES 4–6

Ingredients
1 × 3½lb chicken
3 tbsp freshly grated coconut
2 tbsp vegetable oil
2 shallots, or 1 small onion, finely chopped
2 cloves garlic, crushed

1 piece lemongrass, 2in long
1 piece galingal or fresh ginger, 1in long, peeled and thinly sliced
2 small green chilies, seeded and finely chopped
1 piece shrimp paste, ½in square, or 1 tbsp fish sauce
14fl oz canned coconut milk
1¼ cups chicken stock

2 lime leaves (optional)
1 tbsp sugar
1 tbsp rice or white wine vinegar
2 ripe tomatoes, to garnish
2 tbsp chopped cilantro leaves, to garnish
boiled rice, to serve

1 To joint the chicken, remove the legs and wings with a chopping knife. Skin the pieces and divide the drumsticks from the thighs and, using a pair of kitchen scissors, remove the lower part of the chicken leaving the breast piece. Remove as many of the bones as you can, to make the dish easier to eat. Cut the breast piece into 4 and set aside.

2 Dry-fry the coconut in a large wok until evenly brown. Add the vegetable oil, shallots or onion, garlic, lemongrass, galingal or ginger, chilies, and shrimp paste or fish sauce. Fry briefly to release the flavors. Preheat the oven to 350°F. Add the chicken joints to the wok and brown evenly with the spices for 2–3 minutes.

3 Strain the coconut milk, and add the thin part with the chicken stock, lime leaves if using, sugar, and vinegar. Transfer to a glazed clay pot, cover, and bake for 50–55 minutes or until the chicken is tender. Stir in the coconut milk solids and return to the oven for 5–10 minutes to simmer and thicken.

4 Place the tomatoes in a bowl and cover with boiling water to loosen and remove the skins. Halve the tomatoes, remove the seeds, and cut into large dice. Add the tomatoes to the finished dish, scatter with the chopped cilantro, and serve with a bowl of rice.

Green Vegetable Salad with Coconut Mint Dip

Syabas

This dish is served as an accompaniment to Singapore and Malaysian meat dishes.

SERVES 4–6	4oz bean sprouts	⅓ cup cream of coconut
	lettuce leaves, to serve	2 tsp fish sauce
Ingredients		3 tbsp vegetable oil
4oz snow peas, trimmed, stringed, and halved	**Dipping sauce**	juice of I lime
4oz green beans, trimmed and halved	I clove garlic, crushed	2 tbsp freshly chopped mint
½ hothouse cucumber, halved and sliced	I small green chili, seeded and finely chopped	
4oz Napa cabbage, roughly shredded	2 tsp sugar	

1 Bring a saucepan of salted water to the boil. Blanch the snow peas, beans, and cucumber for 4 minutes. Refresh under cold running water. Drain and set aside.

2 To make the dressing, pound the garlic, chili and sugar together using a pestle and mortar. Add the cream of coconut, fish sauce, vegetable oil, lime juice, and mint.

3 Pour the dressing into a shallow bowl and serve with the salad ingredients arranged in an open basket.

Sizzling Steak

Daging

This method of sizzling meat on a hot grill can also be applied to sliced chicken or pork.

SERVES 4–6	2 tsp whole black peppercorns	**Dipping sauce**
	I tbsp sugar	⅓ cup beef stock
Ingredients	2 tbsp tamarind sauce	2 tbsp tomato ketchup
4 × 7oz rump steaks	3 tbsp dark soy sauce	I tsp chili sauce
I clove garlic, crushed	I tbsp oyster sauce	juice of I lime
I piece fresh ginger, I in long, peeled and finely chopped	vegetable oil, for brushing	

1 Pound and blend all the ingredients together. Pour the marinade over the beef and allow the flavors to mingle for up to 8 hours.

2 Heat a cast-iron skillet over a high heat. Scrape the marinade from the meat and reserve. Brush the meat with oil and cook for 2 minutes on each side, or as you prefer.

3 Place the marinade in a pan, add the stock, sauces and lime juice, and simmer briefly. Serve the steaks and the dipping sauce separately.

CHICKEN SATAY WITH PEANUT SAUCE

Sate Ayam Saos Kacang

Both the marinated chicken and sauce can be stored in the freezer for up to 6 weeks. Allow 2 hours to thaw.

SERVES 4–6

Ingredients
4 boneless, skinless chicken breasts
1 tbsp coriander seeds
2 tsp fennel seeds
2 cloves garlic, crushed
1 piece lemongrass, 2in long, shredded
½ tsp turmeric
2 tsp sugar
½ tsp salt
2 tbsp soy sauce

1 tbsp sesame oil
juice of ½ lime
lettuce leaves, to serve
1 bunch mint leaves, to garnish
1 lime, quartered, to garnish
cucumber sticks, to garnish

Sauce
5oz raw peanuts
1 tbsp vegetable oil
2 shallots, or 1 small onion, finely chopped
1 clove garlic, crushed

1–2 small chilies, seeded and finely chopped
1 piece shrimp paste, ½in square, or 1 tbsp fish sauce
2 tbsp tamarind sauce
½ cup coconut milk
1 tbsp honey

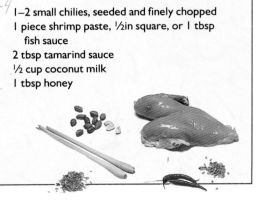

1 Cut the chicken into long thin strips and thread, zig-zag, onto 12 bamboo skewers. Arrange on a flat plate and set aside.

2 To make the marinade, dry-fry the coriander and fennel seeds in a wok. Grind smoothly using a pestle and mortar or food processor, then add to the wok with the garlic, lemongrass, turmeric, sugar, salt, soy sauce, sesame oil, and lime juice. Allow the mixture to cool. Spread it over the chicken and leave in a cool place for up to 8 hours.

3 To make the peanut sauce, fry the peanuts in a wok with a little oil, or place under a moderate broiler, tossing them all the time to prevent burning. Transfer the peanuts to a clean cloth and rub vigorously with your hands to remove the papery skins. Place the peanuts in a food processor and blend for 2 minutes.

4 Heat the vegetable oil in a wok, and soften the shallots or onion, garlic, and chilies. Add the shrimp paste or fish sauce together with the tamarind sauce, coconut milk, and honey. Simmer briefly, add to the peanuts, and process to form a thick sauce. Heat the broiler to moderately hot. If using a barbecue, let the embers settle to a white glow. Brush the chicken with a little vegetable oil and cook for 6–8 minutes. Serve on a bed of lettuce, garnished, together with a bowl of dipping sauce.

HOT CHILI CRAB WITH GINGER AND LIME

Ikan Maris

Serve this dish with a bowl of cucumber sticks and hot slices of toast.

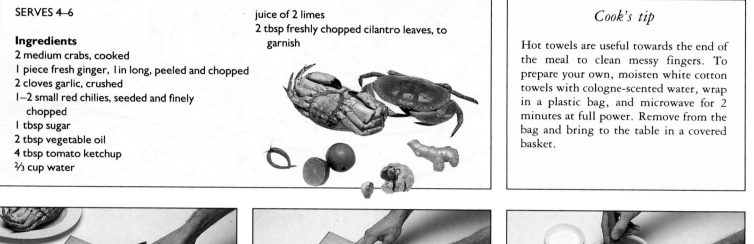

SERVES 4–6

Ingredients

2 medium crabs, cooked
1 piece fresh ginger, 1 in long, peeled and chopped
2 cloves garlic, crushed
1–2 small red chilies, seeded and finely
  chopped
1 tbsp sugar
2 tbsp vegetable oil
4 tbsp tomato ketchup
⅔ cup water
juice of 2 limes
2 tbsp freshly chopped cilantro leaves, to
garnish

Cook's tip

Hot towels are useful towards the end of the meal to clean messy fingers. To prepare your own, moisten white cotton towels with cologne-scented water, wrap in a plastic bag, and microwave for 2 minutes at full power. Remove from the bag and bring to the table in a covered basket.

1 To prepare the crab, twist off the legs and claws. Crack open the thickest part of the shell with a hammer or the back of a knife.

2 Pry off the underside leg section with your two thumbs. From this section, remove the stomach sac and the grey gills, and discard. Cut the section into 4 with a knife. Cut the upper shell into 6 equal pieces.

3 Pound the ginger, garlic, chilies, and sugar using a pestle and mortar. Heat the vegetable oil in a large wok, add the pounded spices, and fry gently for about 1–2 minutes. Add the tomato ketchup, water, and lime juice and simmer briefly.

4 Add the pieces of crab and heat through for 3–4 minutes. Turn out into a serving bowl and scatter with the chopped cilantro.

MALAYSIAN FISH CURRY

Ikan Moolee

Hot Tomato Sambal is often served as an accompaniment to this dish.

SERVES 4–6

Ingredients

1½lb monkfish, hokey, or red snapper fillet
salt, to season
3 tbsp freshly grated or shredded coconut
2 tbsp vegetable oil
1 piece galingal or fresh ginger, 1in long, peeled

and thinly sliced
2 small red chilies, seeded and finely chopped
2 cloves garlic, crushed
1 piece lemongrass, 2in long, shredded
1 piece shrimp paste, ½in square, or 1 tbsp fish sauce
14oz canned coconut milk
2½ cups chicken stock

½ tsp turmeric
3 tsp sugar
juice of 1 lime, or ½ lemon

1 Cut the fish into large chunks, season with salt, and set aside.

2 Dry-fry the coconut in a large wok until evenly brown. Add the vegetable oil, galingal or ginger, chilies, garlic, and lemongrass and fry briefly. Stir in the shrimp paste or fish sauce. Strain the coconut milk, then add the thin coconut milk.

3 Add the chicken stock, turmeric, sugar, a little salt, and the lime or lemon juice. Simmer for 10 minutes. Add the fish and simmer for 6–8 minutes. Stir in the coconut milk solids, simmer gently to thicken, and serve with rice.

PLAIN BOILED RICE

A small amount of vegetable oil added to the rice will enhance its natural flavor.

SERVES 4–6

Ingredients

14oz long-grain rice
1 tbsp vegetable oil
3 cups boiling water
½ tsp salt

1 Wash and drain the rice several times in cold water until the water is no longer starchy. Put the rice in a heavy saucepan, add the vegetable oil, water, and salt. Stir once to prevent the rice from sticking to the pan and simmer for 10–12 minutes. After this time, remove from the heat, cover, and allow the rice to steam in its own heat for another 5 minutes. Fluff the rice with a fork or chopsticks before serving.

COCONUT RICE WITH LEMONGRASS

Serve this rice dish with Sizzling Steak or other meat dishes.

SERVES 4–6

Ingredients

14oz long-grain rice

½ tsp salt
1 piece lemongrass, 2in long
1oz unsweetened cream of coconut
3 cups boiling water

1 Wash and drain the rice several times in cold water until the water is no longer starchy. Put the rice, salt, lemongrass, and cream of coconut in a heavy saucepan, cover with the measured amount of boiling water. Stir once to prevent the grains from sticking, and simmer uncovered for 10–12 minutes.

2 Remove from the heat, cover, and allow to steam in its own heat for a further 5 minutes. Fluff the rice with a fork or chopsticks before serving.

SINGAPORE SLING

Singapore Sling is enjoyed in cocktail bars around the world. Recipes vary considerably, but they all use a standard measure that equates to a little less than 2 tbsp.

SERVES 1

Ingredients
ice
2 measures gin
1 measure cherry brandy

1 measure lemon juice
soda water, to taste
1 slice orange
1 slice lemon
1 Maraschino cherry, to garnish
1 mint sprig, to garnish

1 Wrap the ice in a clean cloth, and crush with a rolling pin or the underside of a saucepan. Half-fill a cocktail shaker with ice.

2 Add the gin, cherry brandy, and lemon juice and shake.

3 Strain the mixture into a goblet or tall glass over ice cubes. Fill with soda water to taste, and decorate with the slices of orange and lemon, and the cherry and mint.

SPECIAL FRIED NOODLES

Mee Goreng

Mee Goreng is perhaps the most well-known dish of Singapore. It is prepared from a wide range of ingredients.

SERVES 4–6

Ingredients
10oz egg noodles
1 skinless chicken breast
4oz lean pork
2 tbsp vegetable oil
6oz shrimp tails, fresh or cooked
4 shallots, or 1 medium onion, chopped
1 piece fresh ginger, ¾in long,
    peeled and thinly sliced
2 cloves garlic, crushed
3 tbsp light soy sauce
1–2 tsp chili sauce
1 tbsp rice or white-wine vinegar
1 tsp sugar
½ tsp salt
4oz Napa cabbage, shredded
4oz fresh spinach, shredded
3 scallions, shredded

1 Bring a large saucepan of salted water to the boil and cook the noodles according to the instructions on the packet. Drain and set aside. Place the chicken breast and pork in the freezer for 30 minutes to firm but not freeze.

2 Slice the meat thinly against the grain. Heat the oil in a large wok and fry the chicken, pork, and shrimp for 2–3 minutes. Add the shallots or onion, ginger, and garlic and fry without letting them color.

3 Add the soy and chili sauces, vinegar, sugar, and salt. Bring to a simmer, add the Napa cabbage, spinach, and scallions, cover, and cook for 3–4 minutes. Lastly add the noodles, heat through, and serve.

BROILED FISH WITH A CASHEW-GINGER MARINADE

Panggang Bungkus

To capture the sweet spicy flavors of this Indonesian favorite, marinated fish are wrapped in green banana leaves or foil and baked. The packets of fish are brought to the table, releasing a sweet spicy aroma.

SERVES 4

Ingredients

2½lb pomfret, parrot fish, or sea bass, scaled and
    cleaned
5oz raw cashew nuts
2 shallots, or 1 small onion, finely chopped
1 piece fresh ginger, ½in long, peeled and finely
    chopped
1 clove garlic, crushed
1 small red chili, seeded and finely chopped
2 tbsp vegetable oil
1 tbsp shrimp paste
2 tsp sugar
½ tsp salt
2 tbsp tamarind sauce
2 tbsp tomato ketchup
juice of 2 limes
4 young banana leaves, or aluminium foil

1 Score the fish 3–4 times on each side with a sharp knife to help it cook through to the bone. Set aside.

2 Grind the cashew nuts, shallots or onion, ginger, garlic, and chili to a fine paste using a pestle and mortar or food processor. Add the vegetable oil, shrimp paste, sugar, and salt and blend, then add the tamarind sauce, tomato ketchup, and lime juice.

Cook's tip

Banana leaves are readily available from Indian or Southeast Asian food stores. However, if these are difficult to obtain, simply wrap each fish in aluminium foil.

For an authentic taste of the Far East, the fish can be barbecued. Light the barbecue and allow the embers to settle to a steady glow. Cook each fish packet for 30–35 minutes.

3 Cover both sides of the fish with the marinade and leave for up to 8 hours to marinate.

4 To soften the banana leaves, remove the thick central stem and immerse the leaves in boiling water for 1 minute. Brush the leaves with vegetable oil. Wrap the fish in a banana leaf fastened with a bamboo skewer. Then preheat the oven to 350°F and bake for 30–35 minutes.

Beef Satay with a Hot Mango Dip

Sate Bali

Serve this dish with a green salad and a bowl of plain rice.

MAKES 12 SKEWERS

Ingredients
1lb sirloin steak, ¾in thick, trimmed
1 tbsp coriander seeds
1 tsp cumin seeds
2oz raw cashew nuts
1 tbsp vegetable oil
2 shallots, or 1 small onion, finely chopped

1 piece fresh ginger, ½in long, peeled and finely chopped
1 clove garlic, crushed
2 tbsp tamarind sauce
2 tbsp dark soy sauce
2 tsp sugar
1 tsp rice or white-wine vinegar

Hot mango dip
1 ripe mango
1–2 small red chilies, seeded and finely chopped
1 tbsp fish sauce
juice of 1 lime
2 tsp sugar
¼ tsp salt
2 tbsp freshly chopped cilantro leaves

1 Slice the beef into long narrow strips and thread, zig-zag, onto 12 bamboo skewers. Lay on a flat plate and set aside.

2 For the marinade, dry-fry the seeds and nuts in a large wok until evenly brown. Place in a pestle and mortar with a rough surface and crush finely. Alternatively, blend the spices and nuts in a food processor. Add the vegetable oil, shallots or onion, ginger, garlic, tamarind and soy sauces, sugar, and vinegar. Spread this mixture over the beef and leave to marinate for up to 8 hours. Cook the beef under a moderate broiler or over a barbecue for 6–8 minutes, turning to ensure an even color. Meanwhile, make the mango dip.

3 Process the mango flesh with the chilies, fish sauce, lime juice, sugar, and salt until smooth, then add the cilantro.

Shrimp Satay with Paw Paw Sauce

Udang Sate

Fresh shrimp are available frozen from reputable fishmongers. Chinese supermarkets also keep a good supply.

MAKES 12 SKEWERS

Ingredients
1½lb whole fresh shrimp tails or 24 jumbo shrimp
2 tbsp coriander seeds
2 tsp fennel seeds
2 shallots, or 1 small onion, finely chopped
1 piece fresh ginger, ½in long, peeled and finely chopped

2 cloves garlic, crushed
1 piece lemongrass, 2in long
2 tsp unsweetened cream of coconut
juice of 1 lime
1 tbsp fish sauce
2 tsp chili sauce
2 tbsp light soy sauce
4 tsp sugar
½ tsp salt

lettuce leaves, to serve

Sauce
2 ripe paw paws or papayas
juice of 1 lime
½ tsp freshly ground black pepper
pinch of salt
2 tbsp freshly chopped mint

1 Thread the shrimp onto 12 bamboo skewers and lay on a flat plate.

2 Dry-fry the coriander and fennel seeds, then pound smoothly in a pestle and mortar. Add the shallots or onion, ginger, garlic, and lemongrass and combine. Lastly add the cream of coconut, lime juice, fish, chili and soy sauces, sugar, and salt. Spread the sauce over the shrimp and leave in a cool place for up to 8 hours. Cook the shrimp under a moderate broiler or over a barbecue for 6–8 minutes, turning once.

3 Blend the paw paw, lime juice, pepper, and salt. Stir in the mint and serve.

SHRIMP CURRY WITH QUAILS' EGGS

Gulai Udang

Quails' eggs are available from speciality food shops and gourmet stores. Hens' eggs may be substituted if quails' eggs are hard to come by. Use 1 hen's egg to every 4 quails' eggs.

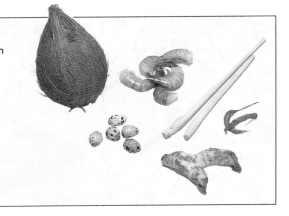

SERVES 4

Ingredients

2lb fresh shrimp tails, peeled and deveined
12 quails' eggs
2 tbsp vegetable oil
4 shallots or 1 medium onion, finely chopped
1 piece galingal or fresh ginger, 1 in long, peeled and chopped
2 cloves garlic, crushed
1 piece lemongrass, 2in long, finely shredded
1–2 small red chilies, seeded and finely chopped

½ tsp turmeric
1 piece shrimp paste, ½in square, or 1 tbsp fish sauce
14fl oz canned coconut milk
1¼ cups chicken stock
4oz Napa cabbage, roughly shredded
2 tsp sugar
½ tsp salt
2 scallions, green part only, shredded, to garnish
2 tbsp shredded coconut, to garnish

1 Boil the quails' eggs for 8 minutes. Refresh in cold water, peel by dipping in cold water to release the shells, and set aside.

2 Heat the vegetable oil in a large wok, add the shallots or onion, galingal or ginger and garlic and soften without coloring. Add the lemongrass, chilies, turmeric, and shrimp paste or fish sauce and fry briefly to bring out their flavors.

3 Add the shrimp and fry briefly. Pour the coconut milk in a strainer over a bowl, then add the thin part of the milk with the chicken stock. Add the Napa cabbage, sugar, and salt and then bring to the boil. Simmer for 6–8 minutes.

4 Turn out onto a serving dish, halve the quails' eggs and toss in the sauce. Scatter with the scallions and the shredded coconut.

BROILED CASHEW NUT CHICKEN

Ayam Bali

This dish comes from the beautiful island of Bali where nuts are widely used as a base for sauces and marinades. Serve with a green salad and a hot chili dipping sauce such as Hot Chili and Garlic Dipping Sauce.

SERVES 4–6

Ingredients
4 chicken legs

Marinade
2oz raw cashew or macadamia nuts
2 shallots, or 1 small onion, finely chopped
2 cloves garlic, crushed
2 small red chilies, chopped
1 piece lemongrass, 2in long
1 tbsp tamarind sauce

2 tbsp dark soy sauce
1 tbsp fish sauce (optional)
2 tsp sugar
½ tsp salt
1 tbsp rice or white wine vinegar
Napa cabbage, to serve
radishes, sliced, to garnish
½ hothouse cucumber, sliced, to garnish

1 Using a sharp knife, slash the chicken legs several times through to the bone, chop off the knuckle end, and set aside.

2 To make the marinade, place the cashew or macadamia nuts in a food processor or coarse pestle and mortar and grind.

3 Add the shallots or onion, garlic, chilies and lemongrass, and blend. Add the remaining marinade ingredients.

4 Spread the marinade over the chicken and leave in a cool place for up to 8 hours. Broil the chicken under a moderate heat or over a barbecue for 15 minutes on each side. Place on a dish lined with Napa cabbage and garnish with the sliced radishes and cucumber.

INDONESIAN PORK AND SHRIMP RICE

Nasi Goreng

Nasi Goreng is an attractive way of using up leftovers and appears in many variations throughout Indonesia. Rice is the main ingredient, although almost anything can be added for color and flavor.

SERVES 4–6

Ingredients
3 eggs
pinch of salt
4 tbsp vegetable oil
6 shallots, or 1 large onion, chopped
2 cloves garlic, crushed
1 piece fresh ginger, 1 in long, peeled and chopped
2–3 small red chilies, seeded and finely chopped
1 tbsp tamarind sauce
1 piece shrimp paste, ½ in square, or 1 tbsp fish sauce
½ tsp turmeric
6 tsp unsweetened cream of coconut
juice of 2 limes
2 tsp sugar
½ tsp salt
12oz lean pork or chicken breasts, skinned and sliced
12oz fresh or cooked shrimp tails, peeled
6oz bean sprouts
6oz Napa cabbage, shredded
6oz frozen peas, thawed
9oz long-grain rice, cooked to make 1½lb
1 small bunch cilantro or basil, roughly chopped, to garnish

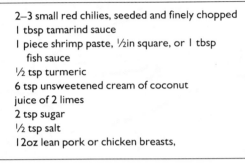

1 In a bowl, beat the eggs with a pinch of salt. Heat a nonstick frying pan over a moderate heat. Pour in the eggs and move the pan around until they begin to set. When set, roll up, slice thinly, cover, and set aside.

2 Heat 1 tbsp of the oil in a wok and fry the shallots or onion until evenly brown. Remove from pan, set aside and keep warm.

3 Heat the remaining 3 tbsp of oil in the wok, add the garlic, ginger and chilies, and soften without coloring. Stir in the tamarind and shrimp paste or fish sauce, turmeric, cream of coconut, lime juice, sugar, and salt. Combine briefly over a moderate heat. Add the pork or chicken and shrimp, and fry for 3–4 minutes.

4 Toss the bean sprouts, Napa cabbage, and peas in the spices and cook briefly. Add the rice and stir-fry for 6–8 minutes, stirring to prevent it from burning. Transfer to a large serving plate, decorate with shredded egg pancake, the fried shallots or onion, and chopped cilantro or basil.

HOT TOMATO SAMBAL

Sambal Tomat

Sambals are placed on the table as a condiment and are used mainly for dipping meat and fish. They are very strong and should be used sparingly.

MAKES ½ CUP

Ingredients
3 ripe tomatoes, cored
½ tsp salt
I tsp chili sauce
4 tbsp fish sauce, or soy sauce
I tbsp chopped cilantro leaves

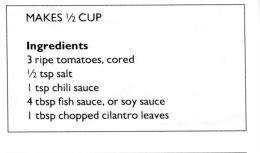

1 Cover the tomatoes with boiling water to loosen the skins. Remove the skins, halve, discard the seeds, and chop finely.

2 Place the chopped tomatoes in a bowl, add the salt, chili sauce, fish sauce or soy sauce, and cilantro.

HOT CHILI AND GARLIC DIPPING SAUCE

Sambal Kecap

This sambal is particularly strong, so warn guests who are unaccustomed to spicy foods.

MAKES ½ CUP

Ingredients
I clove garlic, crushed
2 small red chilies, seeded and finely chopped
2 tsp sugar
I tsp tamarind sauce
4 tbsp soy sauce
juice of ½ lime

1 Pound the garlic, chilies, and sugar until smooth using a pestle and mortar, or grind in a food processor.

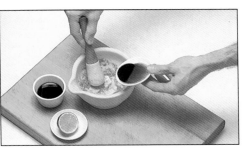

2 Add the tamarind sauce, soy sauce, and lime juice.

CUCUMBER SAMBAL

Sambal Selamat

This sambal has a piquant flavor without the hotness of chilies found in other recipes.

MAKES ⅔ CUP

Ingredients
I clove garlic, crushed
I tsp fennel seeds
2 tsp sugar
½ tsp salt
2 shallots, or I small onion, finely sliced
½ cup rice or white-wine vinegar
¼ hothouse cucumber, finely diced

1 Place the garlic, fennel seeds, sugar, and salt in a pestle and mortar and pound finely. Alternatively, grind the ingredients thoroughly in a food processor.

2 Stir in the shallots or onion, vinegar and cucumber and allow to stand for at least 6 hours to allow the flavors to combine.

SPICY PEANUT RICE CAKES

Rempeyek

Serve these spicy rice cakes with a crisp green salad and a dipping sauce such as Hot Tomato Sambal.

MAKES 16 PIECES

Ingredients
1 clove garlic, crushed
1 piece fresh ginger, ½in long, peeled and finely chopped
¼ tsp turmeric
1 tsp sugar
½ tsp salt
1 tsp chili sauce
2 tsp fish or soy sauce

2 tbsp chopped cilantro leaves
juice of ½ lime
4oz long-grain rice, cooked
raw peanuts, chopped
¼ pint vegetable oil, for deep-frying

1 Pound together the garlic, ginger, and turmeric using a pestle and mortar. Add the sugar, salt, chili and fish or soy sauce, cilantro, and lime juice.

2 Add 3oz of the cooked rice and pound until smooth and sticky. Stir in the remainder of the rice. Wet your hands and shape into thumb-size balls.

3 Roll the balls in chopped peanuts to coat evenly. Then set aside until ready to cook and serve.

4 Heat the vegetable oil in a deep frying pan. Prepare a tray lined with paper towels to drain the rice cakes. Deep-fry 3 cakes at a time until crisp and golden, remove with a slotted spoon, then drain on paper towels.

VEGETABLE SALAD WITH A HOT PEANUT SAUCE

Gado Gado

Serve this vegetable salad with Indonesian Pork and Shrimp Rice and Shrimp Crackers. The peanut sauce is served separately from the salad, and everyone helps themselves.

SERVES 4–6

Ingredients
2 medium potatoes, peeled
6oz green beans, trimmed

Peanut sauce
5oz raw peanuts
1 tbsp vegetable oil
2 shallots, or 1 small onion, finely chopped

1 clove garlic, crushed
1–2 small chilies, seeded and finely chopped
1 piece shrimp paste, ½in square, or 1 tbsp fish sauce (optional)
2 tbsp tamarind sauce
½ cup canned coconut milk
1 tbsp clear honey

Salad ingredients
6oz Napa cabbage, shredded

1 iceberg or bibb lettuce
6oz bean sprouts
½ hothouse cucumber, cut into fingers
5oz giant white radish, shredded
3 scallions
8oz tofu, cut into large dice
3 hard-cooked eggs, quartered
1 small bunch cilantro

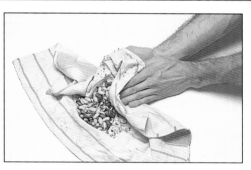

1 Bring the potatoes to the boil in salted water and simmer for 20 minutes. Cook the beans for 3–4 minutes. Drain the potatoes and beans and then refresh under cold running water.

2 For the peanut sauce, dry-fry the peanuts in a wok, or place under a moderate broiler, tossing them all the time to prevent burning. Transfer the peanuts to a clean cloth and rub vigorously with your hands to remove the papery skins. Place the peanuts in a food processor and blend for 2 minutes.

3 Heat the vegetable oil in a wok, and soften the shallots or onion, garlic, and chilies without letting them color. Add the shrimp paste or fish sauce if using, together with the tamarind sauce, coconut milk, and honey. Simmer briefly, add to the peanuts, and process to form a thick sauce.

4 Arrange the salad ingredients, potatoes, and beans on a large platter and serve with a bowl of the peanut sauce.

TABLE-TOP SIMMER POT

Ta Pin Lo

This meal is well-known in many Eastern countries and serves to unite all members of the family. The idea is to cook or reheat a range of ingredients displayed around a pot of simmering chicken stock. The meal is a great social occasion, and each person chooses their own selection of food. Dipping sauces are provided to season the dishes according to taste.

SERVES 4–6

Ingredients
6oz lean pork
6oz beef fillet
1 skinless chicken breast
8oz white fish fillets (monkfish, halibut, or hokey)
8oz tofu
16 fresh shrimp tails, peeled and deveined
7½ cups chicken stock
1 small red chili, split

1 piece fresh ginger, 1in long, peeled and sliced
6oz Chinese egg noodles, uncooked
8oz Napa cabbage, roughly shredded
1 iceberg, bibb, or romaine lettuce, shredded
6 scallions
½ hothouse cucumber, sliced
chili sauce
soy sauce
juice of 3 lemons

1 Place the pork, beef, and chicken in the freezer for 30 minutes to firm but not freeze. Slice the meat thinly and arrange on small side dishes.

2 Skin the fish and cut into thick chunks. Cut the tofu into large cubes and place it with the fish and shrimp tails on a small plate.

3 Bring the chicken stock to the boil with the chili and ginger in a saucepan or casserole that can be served at the table. A flame-lit fondue pot is ideal.

4 Simmer the noodles in a large pan of salted water according to the instructions on the packet. Refresh under cold running water, drain, and place in an attractive bowl.

5 Wash all the salad ingredients in water, drain, and arrange on separate plates.

6 Place the chili sauce, soy sauce, and lemon juice in three separate small dishes suitable for dipping and serve at the table. Fondue forks are ideal for dipping the meat and noodles, tofu, and fish into the stock, although in Singapore little wire baskets are used.

CHICKEN WONTON SOUP WITH SHRIMP

Ji Wun Tun Tang

This soup is a more luxurious version of basic Wonton Soup, and is almost a meal in itself.

SERVES 4	2 scallions, finely chopped	3¾ cups chicken stock
	1 egg	¼ hothouse cucumber, peeled and diced
Ingredients	2 tsp oyster sauce (optional)	1 scallion, roughly shredded, to garnish
11oz skinless chicken breast	salt and pepper	4 sprigs cilantro leaves, to garnish
7oz shrimp tails, fresh or cooked	1 packet wonton skins	1 tomato, skinned, seeded, and diced to garnish
1 tsp finely chopped fresh ginger	1 tbsp cornstarch paste	

1 Place the chicken breast, 5oz shrimp tails, ginger, and scallions in a food processor and mix for 2–3 minutes. Add the egg, oyster sauce, and seasoning and process briefly. Set to one side.

2 Place 8 wonton skins at a time on a surface, moisten the edges with cornstarch paste and place ½ tsp of the filling in the center of each. Fold in half and pinch to seal. Simmer in salted water for 4 minutes.

3 Bring the chicken stock to a boil, add the remaining shrimp tails, and the cucumber and simmer for 3–4 minutes. Add the wontons and simmer to warm through. Garnish and serve hot.

MALACCA FRIED RICE

Chow Fan

There are many versions of this dish throughout the East, all of which make use of leftover rice. Ingredients vary according to what is available, but shrimp are a popular addition.

SERVES 4–6	4 shallots or 1 medium onion, finely chopped	3 scallions, green part only, roughly chopped
	1 tsp finely chopped fresh ginger	8oz thickly sliced roast pork, diced
Ingredients	1 clove garlic, crushed	3 tbsp light soy sauce
2 eggs	8oz shrimp tails, fresh or cooked	12oz long-grain rice, cooked
salt and pepper	1–2 tsp chili sauce (optional)	
3 tbsp vegetable oil	8 oz frozen peas	

1 In a bowl, beat the eggs well and season. Heat 1 tbsp of the oil in a large nonstick frying pan, pour in the eggs, and allow to set without stirring for less than 1 minute. Roll up the pancake, cut into thin strips, and set aside.

2 Heat the remaining vegetable oil in a large wok, add the shallots, ginger, garlic, and shrimp tails and cook for 1–2 minutes; do not let the garlic burn.

3 Add the chili sauce, peas, scallions, pork, and soy sauce. Stir to heat through, then add the rice. Fry the rice over a moderate heat for 6–8 minutes. Transfer to a dish and decorate with the pancake.

PORK AND PEANUT WONTONS WITH PLUM SAUCE

Wanton Goreng

These crispy filled wontons are delicious served with Egg Pancake Salad Wrappers, a popular salad dish of Indonesia. The wontons can be filled and set aside for 8 hours before cooking.

MAKES 40–50 WONTONS

Ingredients
6oz ground pork or sausage meat
2 scallions, finely chopped
2 tbsp peanut butter
2 tsp oyster sauce (optional)
salt and pepper
1 packet wonton skins

2 tbsp flour paste
vegetable oil, for deep-frying

Plum Sauce
8oz dark plum jelly
1 tbsp rice or white-wine vinegar
1 tbsp dark soy sauce
½ tsp chili sauce

1 Combine the ground pork, scallions, peanut butter, oyster sauce, and seasoning and set aside.

2 For the plum sauce, combine the plum jelly, vinegar, soy and chili sauces in a serving bowl and set aside.

3 To fill the wonton skins, place 8 wrappers at a time on a work surface, moisten the edges with the flour paste, and place ½ tsp of the pork mixture on each one. Fold in half, corner to corner, and twist.

4 Fill a wok or deep frying pan one-third with vegetable oil and heat to 385°F. Have a wire strainer or frying basket ready and a tray lined with paper towels. Drop the wontons, 8 at a time, in the hot fat and fry until golden, for about 1–2 minutes. Lift out onto the paper-lined tray and sprinkle with fine salt. Place the plum sauce on a serving plate and surround with the crispy wontons.

HOT CHILI SHRIMP

Udang

Hot Chili Prawns can be prepared about 8 hours in advance and are best broiled or barbecued.

SERVES 4–6

Ingredients
1 clove garlic, crushed
1 piece fresh ginger, ½in long, peeled and chopped
1 small red chili, seeded and chopped
2 tsp sugar
1 tbsp light soy sauce
1 tbsp vegetable oil
1 tsp sesame oil
juice of 1 lime
salt, to taste
1½lb whole shrimp, uncooked
6oz cherry tomatoes
½ hothouse cucumber, cut into chunks
1 small bunch cilantro, roughly chopped

---

1 Pound the garlic, ginger, chili, and sugar to a paste using a pestle and mortar. Add the soy sauce, vegetable and sesame oils, lime juice, and salt. Cover the shrimp with the marinade and allow to marinate for as long as possible, preferable 8 hours.

2 Thread the shrimp, tomatoes, and cucumber onto bamboo skewers. Broil the shrimp for 3–4 minutes, scatter with the cilantro, and serve.

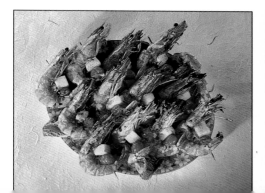

SHRIMP CRACKERS

Krupuk

Shrimp Crackers are a popular addition to many Far Eastern dishes and are often served before guests come to the table. Some supermarkets and food stores sell crackers ready for cooking.

SERVES 4–6

Ingredients
1¼ cups vegetable oil
2oz uncooked shrimp crackers
fine table salt, to taste

1 Line a tray with paper towels. Heat the oil in a large wok until it begins to smoke. Lower the heat to maintain a steady temperature.

2 Drop 3–4 prawn crackers into the oil. Remove from the oil before they begin to color and transfer to the paper-lined tray. Serve sprinkled with salt.

SWEET AND SOUR GINGER SAMBAL

Sambal Jahe

Sambals are a common sight at Indonesian and Malaysian tables. Their purpose is to perk-up or cool down hot chili flavors. Sambals can also include simple components such as onion and cucumber.

MAKES 6 TBSP

Ingredients
4–5 small red chilis, seeded and chopped
2 shallots, or 1 small onion, chopped
2 cloves garlic
1 piece fresh ginger, ¾in long, peeled
2 tbsp sugar
¼ tsp salt
3 tbsp rice or white-wine vinegar

1 Finely pound or grind the chilies and shallots or onion together using a pestle and mortar or food processor.

2 Add the garlic, ginger, sugar, and salt and continue to grind until smooth. Lastly add the vinegar, combine, and pour into an airtight container.

SPICY PORK WITH LEMONGRASS AND COCONUT

Semur Daging

Serve this dish with plain boiled rice and Hot Tomato Sambal.

SERVES 4–6

Ingredients
1 ½lb lean pork
2 tbsp vegetable oil

4 shallots, or 1 medium onion, chopped
1 piece lemongrass, 2in long, finely shredded
1–2 small red chilies, seeded and finely chopped
1 piece shrimp paste, ½in square
14oz canned coconut milk

1 ¼ cups chicken stock
1 tsp sugar
juice of 1 lemon
zest of 1 satsuma, finely shredded
1 small bunch cilantro, chopped

3 Add the coconut milk, chicken stock, sugar, and lemon juice. Return to a boil and simmer for 15–20 minutes. Transfer the pork to a serving dish and sprinkle with the zest of the satsuma and the cilantro.

1 Place the pork in the freezer for 30 minutes. Slice the meat thinly.

2 Heat the vegetable oil in a large wok, add the shallots or onion, lemongrass, chilies, and shrimp paste. Add the pork and seal.

EGG PANCAKE SALAD WRAPPERS

Nonya Popiah

One of Indonesia's favorite snack foods, pancakes are assembled according to taste and dipped in various sauces.

SERVES 4–6

Ingredients
2 eggs
½ tsp salt
1 tsp vegetable oil, plus a little for frying
1 cup all-purpose flour
1 ¼ cups water

1 iceberg or bibb lettuce
4oz bean sprouts

Filling
3 tbsp vegetable oil
1 piece fresh ginger, ½in long, peeled and chopped
1 clive garlic, crushed

1 small red chili, seeded and finely chopped
1 tbsp rice or white-wine vinegar
2 tsp sugar
4oz giant white radish, peeled and grated
1 medium carrot, grated
4oz Napa or white cabbage, shredded
2 shallots or 1 small red onion, thinly sliced

1 Break the eggs into a bowl, add the salt, vegetable oil, and flour and stir until smooth. Do not overmix. Add the water, a little at a time, and strain into a jug. Allow the batter to stand for 15–20 minutes.

2 Moisten a small nonstick frying pan with vegetable oil and heat. Cover the base of the pan with batter and cook for 30 seconds. Turn over and cook briefly. Stack the pancakes on a plate, cover, and keep warm.

3 Heat the oil in a large work, add the ginger, garlic, and chili and fry gently. Add the vinegar, sugar, white radish, carrot, cabbage, and shallots. Cook for 3–4 minutes. Serve with the pancakes and salad.

FILIPINO CHICKEN POT

Puchero

This nourishing main course soup is one of many brought to the Philippines by the Spanish in the sixteenth century. The recipe and method are based on Potajes, a special stew still enjoyed throughout much of Spain. In the Philippines, ingredients vary according to what is available, but the dish still retains much of its original character.

SERVES 4–6

Ingredients

6oz dried white beans
3 chicken legs
1 tbsp vegetable oil
12oz lean pork, diced
1 chorizo (optional)
1 small carrot, peeled and roughly chopped
1 medium onion, roughly chopped
7½ cups water
1 clove garlic, crushed

2 tbsp tomato paste
1 bay leaf
2 chicken stock cubes
12oz sweet potatoes or new potatoes, peeled
2 tsp chili sauce
2 tbsp white-wine vinegar
3 firm tomatoes, skinned, seeded, and chopped
8oz Napa cabbage
salt and freshly ground black pepper
3 scallions, shredded
boiled rice, to serve

1 Soak the beans in plenty of cold water for 8 hours. Drain.

2 Divide the chicken drumsticks from the thighs. Chop off the narrow end of each drumstick and discard.

3 Heat the vegetable oil in a wok or large saucepan, add the chicken, pork, sliced chorizo if using, carrot, and onion, then brown.

4 Drain the white beans, and add with the water, garlic, tomato paste, and bay leaf. Bring to a boil and simmer for 2 hours until the beans are almost tender.

5 Crumble in the chicken stock cubes, add the sweet or new potatoes, and the chili sauce, then simmer for 15–20 minutes until the potatoes are cooked.

6 Add the vinegar, tomatoes, and Napa cabbage, then simmer for 1–2 minutes. Season to taste with salt and pepper. The *Puchero* is intended to provide enough liquid to be served as a first course broth. This is followed by a main course of the meat and vegetables scattered with the shredded scallions. Serve with rice as an accompaniment.

SWEET AND SOUR PORK WITH COCONUT SAUCE

Adobo

Adobo is a popular dish of the Philippines. Typically the meat is tenderized in a marinade before being cooked in coconut milk, shallow-fried, and returned to the sauce. Beef, chicken, and fish Adobos are also popular.

SERVES 4–6	1 tbsp sugar	and roughly chopped
	⅔ cup palm or cider vinegar	salt
Ingredients	2 small bay leaves	½ hothouse cucumber, peeled and cut into sticks
1½lb lean pork, diced	1¼ cups chicken stock	2 firm tomatoes, peeled, seeded, and chopped
1 clove garlic, crushed	2oz unsweetened cream of coconut	1 small bunch chives, chopped
1 tsp paprika	⅔ cup vegetable oil or shortening, for frying	
1 tsp cracked black pepper	1 under-ripe papaya or paw paw, peeled, seeded,	

1 Marinate the pork, garlic, paprika, black pepper, sugar, vinegar, and bay leaves for 2 hours. Add the stock and coconut.

2 Simmer gently for 30–35 minutes, remove pork, and drain. Heat the oil and brown the pork evenly. Remove and drain.

3 Return the pork to the sauce with the papaya or paw paw, season, and simmer for 15–20 minutes. Add garnishes and serve.

NOODLES WITH CHICKEN, SHRIMP, AND HAM

Pansit Guisado

Egg noodles can be cooked up to 24 hours in advance and kept in a bowl of cold water.

SERVES 4–6	2oz canned water chestnuts, sliced	7oz canned baby corn, drained
	1 tbsp light soy sauce	2 limes, cut into wedges, to garnish
Ingredients	2 tbsp fish sauce, or strong chicken stock	1 small bunch cilantro, shredded, to garnish
10oz dried egg noodles	6oz cooked chicken breast, sliced	
1 tbsp vegetable oil	5oz cooked ham, thickly sliced, cut into	
1 medium onion, chopped	short fingers	
1 clove garlic, crushed	8oz shrimp tails, cooked and peeled	
1 piece fresh ginger, peeled and chopped	6oz bean sprouts	

1 Cook the noodles according to the packet. Drain and set aside.

2 Fry the onion, garlic, and ginger until soft. Add the chestnuts, sauces, and meat.

3 Add the noodles, bean sprouts, and corn. Stir-fry for 6–8 minutes.

Braised Beef in a Rich Peanut Sauce

Kari Kari

Like many dishes brought to the Philippines by the Spanish, this slow-cooking Estofado, renamed Kari Kari, retains much of its original charm. Rice and peanuts are used to thicken the juices, yielding a rich glossy sauce.

SERVES 4–6

Ingredients
2lb stewing beef (chuck is best)
2 tbsp vegetable oil
1 tbsp annatto seeds, or 1 tsp paprika and a pinch of turmeric
2 medium onions, chopped

2 cloves garlic, crushed
10oz celeriac or rutabaga, peeled and roughly chopped
1¾ cups beef stock
12oz new potatoes, peeled and cut into large dice
1 tbsp fish or anchovy sauce
2 tbsp tamarind sauce
2 tsp sugar

1 bay leaf
1 sprig thyme
3 tbsp long-grain rice, soaked in water
2oz peanuts or 2 tbsp peanut butter
1 tbsp white-wine vinegar
salt and freshly ground black pepper, to taste

1 Cut the beef into 1in cubes and set aside. Heat the vegetable oil in a flame-proof casserole, add the annatto seeds if using, and stir to color the oil dark red. Remove the seeds with a slotted spoon and discard. If you are not using annatto seeds, paprika and turmeric can be added later.

2 Soften the onions, garlic, and the celeriac or rutabaga in the oil without letting them color. Add the beef and sear to keep in the flavor. If you are not using annatto seeds to redden the sauce, stir the paprika and turmeric in with the beef. Add the beef stock, potatoes, fish or anchovy and tamarind sauces, sugar, bay leaf, and thyme. Bring to a simmer and allow to cook on top of the stove for 2 hours.

3 Cover the rice with cold water and leave to stand for 30 minutes. Roast the peanuts under a hot broiler, if using, then rub the skins off in a clean cloth. Drain the rice and grind with the peanuts or peanut butter using a pestle and mortar, or food processor.

4 When the beef is tender, add 4 tbsp of the cooking liquid to the ground rice and nuts. Blend smoothly and stir into the stew. Simmer gently on the stove to thicken, for about 15–20 minutes. To finish, stir in the wine vinegar and season well with the salt and freshly ground pepper.

SUGAR BREAD ROLLS

Ensaimadas

In the Philippines, pots of coffee and hot milky chocolate are brought out for a special custom called the merienda. Meriendas occur morning and afternoon and call for a lavish display of cakes and breads. Many are flavored with sweet coconut although these delicious rolls of Spanish origin are enriched with butter, eggs, and cheese.

MAKES 10 ROLLS

Ingredients
2⅔ cups white bread flour
1 tsp salt
1 tbsp superfine sugar
⅔ cup lukewarm water

1 tsp dried yeast
3 egg yolks
3 tbsp sweet butter, softened
3oz Cheddar cheese, grated
6 tsp sweet butter, melted
6 tbsp sugar

1 Sift the flour, salt, and superfine sugar into a food processor fitted with a dough blade or an electric mixer fitted with a dough hook, then make a well in the center. Dissolve the yeast in the lukewarm water and pour into the well. Add the egg yolks and leave for a few minutes until bubbles appear on the surface of the liquid.

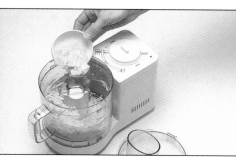

2 Combine the ingredients for less than 1 minute into a firm dough. Add the 2oz of butter and knead until smooth, for about 2–3 minutes, or 4–5 minutes if using an electric mixer. Transfer the dough to a floured bowl, cover, and leave to rise in a warm place until it doubles in volume.

3 Preheat the oven to 375°F. Transfer the dough to a lightly floured work surface and divide into 10 pieces. Spread the grated cheese over the surface and roll each of the pieces into 5in lengths. Coil into snail shapes and place on a lightly greased, high-sided tray or pan measuring 12 × 8in.

4 Cover the tray with a loose-fitting plastic bag and leave to rise for a second time until the dough doubles in volume, for about 45 minutes, or up to 2 hours if conditions are not warm. Bake for 20–25 minutes. Brush with the melted butter, sprinkle with the sugar and allow to cool. Break up the rolls and serve in a lined basket.

SWEET AND SOUR PORK AND SHRIMP SOUP

Sinegang

This main course soup has a sour, rich flavor. Under-ripe fruits and vegetables provide a special tartness.

SERVES 4–6		
Ingredients 12oz lean pork, diced 8oz raw or cooked shrimp tails, peeled 2 tbsp tamarind sauce juice of 2 limes 1 small green guava, peeled, halved, and seeded	1 small, under-ripe mango, peeled, flesh removed, and chopped 6¼ cups chicken stock 1 tbsp fish or soy sauce 10oz sweet potato, peeled and cut into even pieces 8oz unripe tomatoes, quartered 4oz green beans, trimmed and halved	1 star fruit, thickly sliced 3oz green cabbage, shredded salt 1 tsp crushed black pepper 2 scallions, shredded, to garnish 2 limes, quartered, to garnish

1 Trim the pork, peel the shrimp, and set aside. Measure the tamarind sauce and lime juice into a saucepan.

2 Add the pork, guava, and mango. Pour in the stock. Add the fish or soy sauce and simmer, uncovered, for 30 minutes.

3 Add the remaining fruit, vegetables, and shrimp. Simmer for 10–15 minutes. Adjust seasoning, garnish, and serve.

SAVORY PORK PIES

Empanadas

These are native to Galicia in Spain and were brought to the Philippines in the sixteenth century.

MAKES 12 PASTRIES

Ingredients
12oz frozen pastry, thawed

Filling
1 tbsp vegetable oil
1 medium onion, chopped
1 clove garlic, crushed
1 tsp thyme
4oz ground pork
1 tsp paprika
salt and freshly ground black pepper
1 hard cooked egg, chopped
1 medium pickle, chopped
2 tbsp freshly chopped parsley
vegetable oil, for deep-frying

1 To make the filling, heat the vegetable oil in a frying pan or wok and soften the onions, garlic, and thyme without browning, for about 3–4 minutes. Add the pork and paprika, then brown evenly for 6–8 minutes. Season well, transfer to a bowl and cool. When the mixture is cool, add the hard cooked egg, pickle, and parsley.

2 Transfer the pastry to a floured work surface and roll out to a 15in square. Cut out 12 circles 5in in diameter. Place 1 tbsp of the filling on each circle, moisten the edges with a little water, fold over, and seal. Heat the vegetable oil in a deep-fryer, fitted with a basket, to 385°F. Place 3 Empanadas at a time in the basket and deep-fry until golden brown. Frying should take at least 1 minute or the inside filling will not be heated through. Serve warm in a basket covered with a napkin.

SWEET POTATO AND PUMPKIN SHRIMP CAKES

Ukoy

These delicious fried cakes should be served warm with a fish sauce or a dark soy sauce.

SERVES 4–6	½ tsp dried yeast	½ tsp chili sauce
	¾ cup lukewarm water	1 clove garlic, crushed
Ingredients	1 egg, beaten	juice of ½ lime
7oz fresh shrimp tails, peeled and	5oz sweet potato, peeled and grated	vegetable oil, for deep-frying
roughly chopped	8oz pumpkin, peeled, seeded, and grated	
7oz white bread flour	2 scallions, chopped	
½ tsp salt	2oz water chestnuts, sliced and chopped	

1 Sift the flour and salt into a mixing bowl and make a well in the center. Dissolve the yeast in the water, then pour into the well. Pour in the egg and leave for a few minutes until bubbles appear. Mix to a batter.

2 Place the peeled shrimp in a saucepan and cover with water. Bring to a boil and simmer for 10–12 minutes. Drain and refresh in cold water. Roughly chop and set aside. Add the sweet potato and pumpkin.

3 Then add the scallions, water chestnuts, chili sauce, garlic, lime juice, and shrimp. Heat a little oil in a large frying pan. Spoon in the batter in small heaps and fry until golden. Drain and serve.

FILIPINO HOT CHOCOLATE

Napalet a Chocolate

This luxurious hot chocolate is served for merienda with Sugar Bread Rolls or Coconut Rice Fritters.

SERVES 2

Ingredients
2 tbsp sugar
½ cup water
4oz best-quality semi-sweet chocolate
scant 1 cup evaporated milk

1 Measure the sugar and water into a nonstick saucepan. Simmer to make a basic syrup.

2 Break the chocolate into even pieces, add to the syrup, and stir until melted.

3 Add the evaporated milk, return to a simmer, and whisk to a froth. Divide between 2 tall mugs and serve.

COCONUT RICE FRITTERS

Puto

These delicious fritters can be served any time, with a mug of steaming coffee or chocolate.

MAKES 28 FRITTERS

Ingredients
5oz long-grain rice, cooked
2 tbsp coconut milk powder
3 tbsp sugar
2 egg yolks
juice of ½ lemon
3oz shredded coconut
oil, for deep-frying
confectioners' sugar, for dusting

1 Place 3oz of the cooked rice in a pestle and mortar and pound until smooth and sticky. Alternatively, use a food processor. Transfer to a large bowl, combine with the remainder of the rice, the coconut milk powder, sugar, egg yolks, and lemon juice. Spread the shredded coconut onto a tray, divide the mixture into thumb-size pieces with wet hands, and then roll in the coconut into neat balls.

2 Heat a wok or deep-fat fryer fitted with a wire basket to 350°F. Fry the coconut rice balls, 3–4 at a time, for 1–2 minutes until the coconut is evenly brown. Transfer to a plate, and dust with confectioners' sugar. Place a wooden skewer in each fritter and serve with café au lait or hot chocolate at merienda time.

BEEF AND VEGETABLES IN A TABLE-TOP BROTH

Shabu Shabu

Shabu Shabu is the perfect introduction to Japanese cooking and is well suited to party gatherings. The name refers to the swishing sound made as wafer-thin slices of beef, tofu, and vegetables cook in a special broth.

SERVES 4–6

Ingredients
1lb beef sirloin, trimmed
7½ cups water
½ sachet of instant Dashi powder, or ½ vegetable stock cube
5oz carrots
6 scallions, trimmed and sliced
5oz Napa cabbage, roughly shredded
8oz giant white radish, peeled and shredded

10oz Udon, or fine wheat noodles, cooked
4oz canned bamboo shoots, sliced
6oz tofu, cut into large dice
10 shiitake mushrooms, fresh or dried

Sesame dipping sauce
2oz sesame seeds, or 2 tbsp tahini paste
½ cup instant Dashi stock, or vegetable stock
4 tbsp dark soy sauce
2 tsp sugar

2 tbsp sake (optional)
2 tsp Wasabi powder (optional)

Ponzu dipping sauce
⅓ cup lemon juice
1 tbsp rice or white-wine vinegar
⅓ cup dark soy sauce
1 tbsp Tamari sauce
1 tbsp Mirin, or 1 tsp sugar
¼ tsp instant Dashi powder, or ¼ vegetable stock cube

1 Place the meat in the freezer for 30 minutes until firm but not frozen. Slice the meat with a large knife or cleaver. Arrange neatly on a plate, cover, and set aside. Bring the water to a boil in a Japanese donabe, or any other covered flame-proof casserole that is unglazed on the outside. Stir in the Dashi powder or stock cube, cover, and simmer for 8–10 minutes. Serve at the table standing on its own heat source.

2 To prepare the vegetables, bring a saucepan of salted water to the boil. Peel the carrots and with a canelle knife cut a series of grooves along their length. Slice the carrots thinly and blanch for 2–3 minutes. Blanch the scallions, Napa cabbage, and giant white radish for the same time. Arrange the vegetables with the noodles, bamboo shoots, and tofu. Slice the mushrooms (soak dried mushrooms in boiling water for 3–4 minutes).

3 To make the sesame dipping sauce, dry-fry the sesame seeds, if using, in a heavy frying pan, taking care not to burn them. Grind the seeds smoothly using a pestle and mortar with a rough surface. Alternatively, you can use tahini paste.

4 Add the remaining ingredients, combine well, then pour into a shallow dish. Sesame dipping sauce will keep in the refrigerator for 3–4 days.

5 To make the Ponzu dipping sauce, put the ingredients into a screw-top jar and shake well. Provide guests with chopsticks and individual bowls, so they can help themselves to what they want. Towards the end of the meal, each guest takes a portion of noodles and ladles the well-flavored stock over them.

Cook's tip

Dashi is the name given to Japan's most common stock. The flavour derives from a special seaweed known as kelp. This light-tasting stock is available in powder form from oriental food stores. Diluted vegetable stock cube is a good substitute for Dashi.

Tahini paste is a purée of toasted sesame seeds that is used mainly in Middle Eastern cooking. It is available in large supermarkets and specialist food shops.

MISO BREAKFAST SOUP

Miso-shiru

Miso is a fermented bean paste that adds richness and flavor to many of Japan's favorite soups. This soup provides a nourishing start to the day. Miso paste is widely available in health food stores.

MAKES 5 CUPS	5 cups Dashi, or light vegetable stock
	4 tbsp Miso
Ingredients	4oz tofu, cut into large dice
3 shiitake mushrooms, fresh or dried	I scallion, green part only, sliced

1 Slice the mushrooms thinly. If they are dried, soak them first in boiling water for 3–4 minutes. Set aside.

2 Bring the Dashi or light vegetable stock to a boil. Stir in the Miso, add the mushrooms, and simmer for 5 minutes.

3 Ladle the broth into 4 soup bowls and place the tofu in each. Add the scallion and serve.

CRAB AND TOFU DUMPLINGS

Kami-dofu Iridashi

These little crab and ginger dumplings are served as a delicious side accompaniment.

MAKES 30	¼ tsp salt	**Dipping sauce**
	2 tsp light soy sauce	½ cup Dashi, or light vegetable
Ingredients	2 tbsp scallion, green part only, finely chopped	stock
4oz frozen white crabmeat, thawed	I piece fresh ginger, ¾in long, peeled and grated	3 tbsp Mirin, or I tbsp sugar
4oz tofu, drained	vegetable oil, for deep-frying	3 tbsp dark soy sauce
I egg yolk	2oz giant white radish, finely grated	
2 tbsp rice flour, or wheat flour		

1 Squeeze as much moisture out of the crabmeat as you can before using. Press the tofu through a fine strainer with the back of a spoon and then combine with the crabmeat in a bowl.

2 Add the egg yolk, rice flour, salt, scallion, ginger, and soy sauce to the tofu and crabmeat and stir to form a light paste. Set aside. To prepare the dipping sauce, combine the Dashi or stock with the Mirin or sugar and soy sauce.

3 Line a tray with paper towels. Heat the vegetable oil to 385°F. Shape the mixture to make thumb-size pieces. Fry 6 at a time for 1–2 minutes. Drain on the paper. Serve with the sauce and radish.

BARBECUE-GLAZED CHICKEN SKEWERS

Yakitori

Yakitori is popular throughout Japan and is often served as an appetizer with drinks.

MAKES 12 SKEWERS AND 8 WING PIECES

Ingredients
4 chicken thighs, skinned
4 scallions, blanched and cut into short lengths
8 chicken wings

Basting sauce
4 tbsp sake
1/3 cup dark soy sauce
2 tbsp Tamari sauce
3 tbsp Mirin, or sweet sherry
4 tbsp sugar

1 Bone the chicken thighs and cut the meat into large dice. Thread the scallions and chicken onto 12 skewers.

2 To prepare the chicken wings, remove the wing tip at the first joint. Chop through the second joint, revealing the two narrow bones. Take hold of the bones with a clean cloth and pull, turning the meat around the bones inside out. Remove the smaller bone and set aside.

3 Measure the basting sauce ingredients into a stainless steel or enamel saucepan and simmer until reduced by two-thirds. Cool. Heat the broiler to a moderately high temperature. Broil the skewers without applying any oil. When juices begin to emerge from the chicken, baste liberally with the basting sauce. Allow 3 minutes more for the chicken on skewers and not more than 5 minutes for the wings.

RAW FISH AND RICE PARCELS

Sushi

Sushi is something of an art form in Japan, but with a little practice it is possible to make sushi at home.

MAKES 8–10

Ingredients

Tuna sushi
3 sheets nori (paper-thin seaweed)
5oz freshest tuna fillet, cut into fingers
1 tsp Wasabi, made into a thin paste
    with a little water
6 young carrots, blanched
1lb cooked sushi rice

Salmon sushi
2 eggs
1/2 tsp salt
2 tsp sugar
5 sheets nori
1lb cooked sushi rice
5oz freshest salmon fillet, cut into fingers
1 tsp Wasabi, made into a thin paste
    with a little water
1/2 small cucumber, cut into strips

1 To make the tuna sushi, spread half a sheet of nori onto a bamboo mat, lay strips of tuna across the full length and season with the thinned Wasabi. Place a line of blanched carrot next to the tuna and roll tightly. Moisten the edge with water and seal. Place a square of damp wax paper onto the bamboo mat, then spread evenly with sushi rice. Place the seaweed-wrapped tuna along the center and wrap tightly, enclosing the seaweed completely. Remove the paper and cut into neat rounds with a wet knife.

2 To make the salmon sushi, make a simple flat omelete by beating together the eggs, salt and sugar. Heat a large nonstick pan, pour in the egg mixture, stir briefly, and allow to set. Transfer to a clean cloth and cool. Place the nori onto a bamboo mat, cover with the omelete, and trim to size. Spread a layer of rice over the omelete then lay strips of salmon across the width. Season the salmon with the thinned Wasabi, then place a strip of cucumber next to the salmon. Fold the bamboo mat in half, forming a tear shape inside. Cut into neat sections with a wet knife.

SALT-BROILED MACKEREL

Shio-yaki

Shio-yaki means salt-broiled. In Japan, salt is applied to oily fish before cooking to draw out the flavors. Mackerel, garfish, and snapper are the most popular choices, all of which develop a unique flavor and texture when treated with salt. The salt is washed away before cooking.

SERVES 2	Soy-ginger dip	Japanese horseradish
	4 tbsp dark soy sauce	3 tsp Wasabi powder
Ingredients	2 tbsp sugar	2 tsp water
2 small or 1 large mackerel, snapper, or garfish, gutted and cleaned, with head on	1 piece fresh ginger, 1 in long, peeled and finely grated	1 medium carrot, peeled and shredded
2 tbsp fine sea salt		

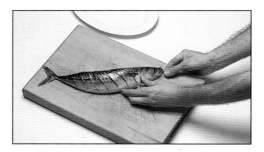

1 Rinse the fish under cold running water and dry well with paper towels. Score the fish several times on each side, cutting down as far as the bone. This will ensure that the fish will cook evenly. Salt the fish inside and out, rubbing well into the skin. Place the fish on a plate and leave to stand for 40 minutes.

2 To make the soy-ginger dip, place the soy sauce, sugar, and ginger in a stainless steel saucepan. Simmer for 2–3 minutes, strain, and cool. To make the Japanese horseradish, measure the Wasabi powder into a small cup, add the water, and stir to make a stiff paste. Shape into a neat ball and place on a heap of shredded carrot.

3 Wash the fish in plenty of cold water to remove the salt. Secure each fish in a curved position before grilling. To do this, pass two bamboo skewers through the length of the fish, one above the eye and one below.

4 Preheat a broiler or barbecue to a moderate temperature and cook the fish for 10–12 minutes, turning once. It is customary to cook the fish plainly, but you may like to baste the skin with a little of the soy-ginger dip halfway through cooking.

EGGPLANT WITH SESAME CHICKEN

Nasu Hasami-age

Young vegetables are prized in Japan for their sweet, delicate flavor. Here, small eggplant are stuffed with seasoned chicken.

SERVES 4

Ingredients
6oz chicken, breast or thigh, skinned
1 scallion, green part only, finely chopped
1 tbsp dark soy sauce
1 tbsp Mirin, or sweet sherry
½ tsp sesame oil
¼ tsp salt
4 small eggplant, about 4in long

1 tbsp sesame seeds
all-purpose flour, for dusting

Dipping sauce
vegetable oil, for deep-frying
4 tbsp dark soy sauce
4 tbsp Dashi, or vegetable stock
3 tbsp Mirin, or sweet sherry

1 To make the stuffing, remove the chicken meat from the bone and grind it finely in a food processor, for about 1–2 minutes. Add the scallion, soy sauce, Mirin or sherry, sesame oil, and salt.

2 Make 4 slits in the eggplant so they remain joined at the stem. Spoon the ground chicken into the eggplant, opening them slightly to accommodate the mixture. Dip the fat end of the stuffed eggplant in the sesame seeds, then dust in flour. Set aside.

3 For the dipping sauce, combine the soy sauce, Dashi or stock, and Mirin or sherry. Pour into a shallow bowl and set aside.

4 Heat the vegetable oil in a deep-fryer to 385°F. Fry the eggplant, 2 at a time, for 3–4 minutes. Lift out with a slotted spoon onto paper towels.

Japanese Rice and Sushi Rice

Sushi-meshi

The Japanese prefer their rice slightly sticky so that it can be shaped and eaten with chopsticks. Authentic Japanese rice can be difficult to obtain in the West, but may be replaced by Thai or long-grain rice, washed only once to retain a degree of stickiness.

YIELDS 2LB COOKED RICE

Ingredients
12oz Japanese, Thai, or long-grain rice
5 cups boiling water
1 piece giant kelp, 2in square (optional)

Dressing
3 tbsp rice vinegar or distilled white vinegar
3 tbsp sugar
2 tsp sea salt

1 If using Japanese rice, wash several times until the water runs clear. Wash Thai or long-grain rice only once and drain well. Place the rice in a large heavy saucepan, cover with the measured amount of water and the kelp, if using. Stir once and simmer, uncovered, for 15 minutes. Turn off the heat, cover, and stand for 5 minutes more to allow the rice to finish cooking in its own steam. Before serving, the rice should be fluffed with a rice paddle or spoon. This rice is a Japanese staple.

2 To prepare sushi rice, make the dressing, by heating the vinegar in a small saucepan, with a lid to keep in the strong vapors. Add the sugar and salt and dissolve. Allow to cool. Spread the cooked rice onto a mat or tray and allow to cool.

3 Pour on the dressing and fluff with a rice paddle or spoon. Keep covered until ready to use.

BATTERED FISH, SHRIMP AND VEGETABLES

Tempura

Tempura is one of the few dishes brought to Japan from the West. The idea came via Spanish and Portuguese missionaries who settled in southern Japan in the late sixteenth century.

SERVES 4–6

Ingredients
I sheet nori
8 large uncooked shrimp tails
6oz whiting or monkfish fillet, cut into fingers
I small eggplant
4 scallions, trimmed
6 shiitake mushrooms, fresh or dried
all-purpose flour, for dusting
vegetable oil, for deep-frying
fine salt, to sprinkle
5 tbsp soy, or Tamari sauce, to serve

Batter
2 egg yolks
I ¼ cups ice water
8oz all-purpose flour
½ tsp salt

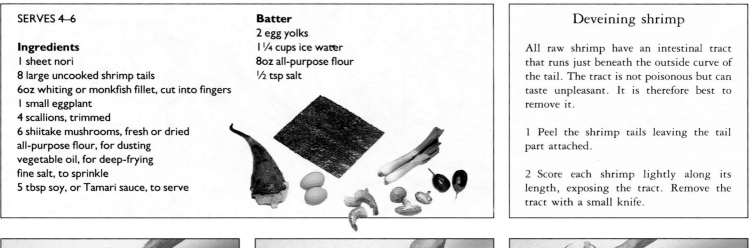

Deveining shrimp

All raw shrimp have an intestinal tract that runs just beneath the outside curve of the tail. The tract is not poisonous but can taste unpleasant. It is therefore best to remove it.

1 Peel the shrimp tails leaving the tail part attached.

2 Score each shrimp lightly along its length, exposing the tract. Remove the tract with a small knife.

1 Cut the nori into ½in strips, 2in long. Moisten one end of the nori with water, and wrap around the tail end of each shrimp. Skewer the shrimp through their length to straighten them. Skewer the fillets of white fish and set aside.

2 Slice the eggplant into neat sections, sprinkle with salt, layer on a plate, and press lightly with your hand to expel the bitter juices. Leave for 20–30 minutes, then rinse under cold water. Dry well and place on bamboo skewers. Prepare the other vegetables on skewers and set aside.

3 The batter should be made just before it is used. Beat the egg yolks and half the ice water together in a bowl, sift in the flour and salt, and stir loosely with chopsticks without mixing into a dry paste. Add the remainder of the water and stir to make a smooth batter. Avoid overmixing.

4 Heat the vegetable oil in a deep-fryer or wok, fitted with a wire draining rack, to 350°F. Dust the fish and vegetables in flour, not more than 3 at a time. Dip into the batter, coating well, then fry in the hot oil until crisp and golden, for about 1–2 minutes. Drain well, sprinkle with fine salt, and drain on paper towels before serving with a soy or Tamari dipping sauce.

STRAW NOODLE SHRIMP IN A SWEET GINGER DIP

Age-mono

Shrimp are a popular feature in Japanese cooking. Rarely are they more delicious than when wrapped in crispy noodles and seaweed.

SERVES 4–6	2 sheets nori	**Dipping sauce**
	12 large fresh shrimp tails, peeled and deveined	6 tbsp soy sauce
Ingredients	vegetable oil, for deep-frying	2 tbsp sugar
3oz Somen noodles, or vermicelli		1 piece fresh ginger, ¾in long, grated

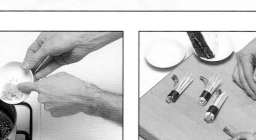

1 Cover the Somen noodles, if using, with boiling water and soak for 1–2 minutes. Drain and dry thoroughly with paper towels. Cut the noodles into 3in lengths. If using vermicelli, cover with boiling water for 1–2 minutes to soften. Cut the nori into ½in strips, 2in long, and set aside. To make the dipping sauce, bring the soy sauce to a boil with the sugar and ginger. Simmer for 2–3 minutes, strain, and cool.

2 Line up the noodles or vermicelli on a wooden board. Roll the shrimp in the noodles so that they adhere in neat strands. Moisten one end of the nori and secure the noodles at the fat end of the shrimp. Set aside.

3 Heat the vegetable oil in a deep-frying pan, or wok fitted with a wire draining rack, to 350°F. Fry the shrimp in the oil, 2 at a time, until the noodles or vermicelli are crisp and golden.

4 To finish, cut through the band of nori with a sharp knife exposing a clean section of shrimp. Drain on paper towels and serve with the dipping sauce in a small dish.

SWEET POTATO AND CHESTNUT CANDIES

Okashi

It is customary in Japan to offer special bean paste candies with tea. The candies tend to be very sweet by themselves, but contrast well with Japanese green teas; in particular, large-leaf Sencha and Banch.

MAKES 18

Ingredients
1lb sweet potato, peeled and roughly chopped
¼ tsp salt
2 egg yolks

7oz sugar
4 tbsp water
5 tbsp rice flour or all-purpose flour
1 tsp orange flower or rose water (optional)
7oz canned chestnuts in heavy syrup, drained
superfine sugar, for dusting

2 strips candied angelica
2 tsp plum or apricot preserves
3–4 drops red food coloring

1 Place the sweet potatoes in a heavy saucepan, cover with cold water, and add the salt. Bring to a boil and simmer until the sweet potatoes are tender, for about 20–25 minutes. Drain well and return to the pan. Mash the sweet potatoes well, or force through a fine strainer. Place the egg yolks, sugar, and water in a small bowl, then combine the flour and orange flower or rose water if using. Add to the purée and stir over a gentle heat to thicken for about 3–4 minutes. Transfer the paste to a tray and cool.

2 To shape the sweet potato paste, place 2 tsp of the mixture into the center of a wet cotton napkin or handkerchief. Enclose the paste in the cotton and twist into a nut shape. If the mixture sticks, ensure the fabric is sufficiently wet.

3 To prepare the chestnuts, rinse away the thick syrup and dry well. Roll the chestnuts in superfine sugar and decorate with strips of angelica. To finish the sweet potato candies, color the plum or apricot preserves with red coloring and decorate each one with a spot of color. Serve in a Japanese lacquer box or on an open plate.

Cook's tip

Sugar-coated chestnuts will keep for up to 5 days at room temperature, stored in a sealed box. Sweet potato candies will also keep, sealed and refrigerated.

TASTE OF INDIA

RAFI FERNANDEZ

The vast sub-continent of India offers a range of culinary delights as rich and diverse as its people and history. Each region has its own unique cooking style: cream, yogurt, ghee, and nuts feature in dishes in the north, while the south favours chilies, coconut, and coconut oil. Fish and mustard oil predominate in the east while the west has incorporated the greatest number of foreign ingredients. One element unites these diverse styles — the use of spices to create the flavors and aromas distinctive of Indian cuisine.

THE PRINCIPLES OF INDIAN COOKING

The Indian diet is the product of many influences – economic, religious, and environmental, but any Indian meal will skilfully combine nutrition with a harmonious blend of textures and flavors. For this reason, care must be taken to provide the correct accompaniment to any dish. Cooling elements such as raithas and salads should be served with hot curries, with pickles and chutneys providing the perfect foil to heavily spiced dishes. There is no myth to Indian cooking. Each of the dishes in this book can be easily prepared in the Western kitchen, and the majority of ingredients are readily available in supermarkets.

EQUIPMENT AND UTENSILS

Chappati griddle (tava) (1) These are made from heavy wrought iron and allow chappatis and other breads to be cooked without burning.
Chappati rolling board (roti takta) (2) This board consists of a round wooden surface on stubby legs and helps in shaping different sizes of breads. The extra height helps disperse excess dry flour.
Chappati rolling pin (velan) (3) These are thinner in shape than Western pins and come in a variety of sizes. Use whichever best suits your hand.
Chappati spoon (roti chamcha) (4) The square-shaped flat head assists in roasting breads on the hot griddle.
Colander (channi) (5) Use a sturdy, stainless steel colander as it will not discolor.
Food processor (6) This is an essential piece of equipment. Small quantities of ingredients can be ground using a pestle and mortar or a coffee grinder.
Heat diffuser (7) Many curries are simmered gently over a low heat, and a heat diffuser helps prevent burning on the base.
Indian frying pan (karai) (8) A karai is similar to a wok but is more rounded in shape and made of heavier metal.
Knives (churrie) (9) Keep knives very sharp. It will be easier to chop ingredients and will ensure neat edges.
Oblong grinding stone and pin (sil padi) (10) This is a traditional Indian 'food processor'. The ingredients are placed on a stone made of heavy slate marked with notches. The rolling pin is used to pulverize the ingredients against the stone.
Rice spoon (chawal ke chamchi) (11) This helps prevent the rice grains from being damaged while serving.
Sizzler (garam thali) (12) This enables food to be served at the table still cooking.
Slotted spoon (channi chamchi) (13) This enables items to be removed safely from deep hot oil or other liquids.
Stainless steel pestle and mortar (hamam dasta) (14) This is ideal for grinding small amounts of wet ingredients such as ginger and garlic. The steel is everlasting and will not retain the strong flavors of the spices.
Stone pestle and mortar (pathar hamam dasta) (15) This is suitable for mixing small amounts of ingredients, both wet and dry.

SPICES

Aniseed (1) This has a delicate liquorice flavor and sweet seeds. It is a good aid to digestion.
Bay leaves (2) Bay leaves feature in a lot of dishes from the north of India. They are also used in aromatic rice.
Black cardamom (3) These large black pods are used whole. They have a menthol aroma and are used mainly in cooking from the north of India.
Black cumin (4) These aromatic seeds are used mainly whole sprinkled on breads and in rice dishes. Do not substitute with ordinary cumin seeds.
Chili powder (5) Many brands are now available and each vary in spiciness. Add small quantities at a time and adjust accordingly.
Cinnamon bark (6) This is also available in stick form. It can be removed from the dish before serving.
Cloves (7) Cloves are used in both savory and sweet dishes.
Coriander, ground (8) Ground coriander not only adds flavor but is also used to thicken curries.
Coriander seeds (9) Coriander seeds are very rarely used whole. Dry-roast the seeds before grinding. Coriander is essential to a good curry.
Cumin, ground (10) Highly aromatic ground cumin is one of the essential ingredients in curries.
Cumin seeds (11) Whole cumin seeds are used mainly in vegetarian dishes. Dry-roast the seeds before grinding.
Fennel seeds (12) The seeds of the fennel are aromatic and sweet. They may be used whole or ground. They are also dry-roasted, cooled and served after meals to aid digestion and freshen the mouth.
Fenugreek powder (13) This slightly bitter-tasting ingredient must be used sparingly.
Fenugreek seeds (14) These are used whole in vegetarian dishes. When planted the seed produces a spinach.
Five-spice powder (15) This is a combination of star anise, fennel, cinnamon, clove, and Sichuan pepper.
Garam masala (16) This combination of spices provides heat to the body and enhances curries. Several combinations are available.
Green cardamom (17) Green cardamom is sweet and aromatic in flavor and is used in both savory and sweet dishes.

Mustard seeds (18) Mustard seeds are odorless but become very pungent when pounded or moistened. When planted they produce mustard spinach.
Nigella (19) Nigella is an aromatic spice with a sharp and tingling taste. It is used mainly in vegetarian dishes.
Onion seeds (20) These black teardrop-shaped seeds have an earthy aroma. They are sprinkled on breads and used in vegetarian dishes.
Peppercorns (21) Peppercorns were introduced to India by the Portuguese and are now an indispensable ingredient in much Indian cooking.
Red chilies (22) Red chilies were introduced to India by the Portuguese. The larger the chili the less hot it is. Remove the seeds for a milder chili taste.
Round red chilies (23) These are hot, with a pimento flavor, and are delicious in pickles.
Saffron (24) Saffron is the world's most expensive spice, produced from the stigma of a particular variety of crocus. Over 100,000 crocus blossoms picked by hand are needed to produce 1lb of saffron.
Star anise (25) Star anise is a star-shaped, liquorice-flavored pod.
Turmeric (26) Turmeric is yellow in color with an earthy but pungent taste. It should be used with caution.

INGREDIENTS

Almond flakes (1) Almond flakes are extremely rich in vitamin B1. They are prohibitively expensive in India.
Apricots (2) Apricots are used mainly for festive occasions and celebrations. Stewed apricots are served with custard as a favorite dessert.
Asafoetida (3) This is a resin with an acrid and bitter taste and a strong odor. Store in a jar with a strong airtight seal to prevent the smell dispersing into other ingredients.
Basmati rice (5) Basmati rice is the staple grain of India. Many brands are now available in the West.
Bengal gram (6) Bengal gram is used whole in lentil curries. The flour (besan) is used to prepare bhajias and may be used to flavor and thicken certain curries.
Black-eyed beans (7) These are oval-shaped beige beans with a distinctive dark 'eye'. They are very popular in the north of India.
Black gram (8) Black gram may be used whole or split. The flour is used to make papadums.
Bottle gourd (9) The fruit of the bottle gourd is whitish-green. Remove peel and pith before using.
Chick peas (garbanzo beans) (10) These are beige, heart-shaped peas, sold dry or cooked in brine. Pre-cooked, chick peas (garbanzo beans) save a lot of preparation time.
Cilantro leaves (11) Cilantro is India's most popular herb, and is well-loved for its refreshing and unique taste and aroma.
Curry leaves (12) Curry leaves are most popular in the south of India. The leaves freeze well without any special preparation.
Eggplant (2) Immerse eggplant in water immediately after cutting to prevent discoloration.
Gentleman's toes (tindla) (13) These tender fruits look like mini cucumbers when cut. If over-ripe they will be red inside.
Ginger (14) Fresh ginger is essential to Indian cuisine and is used in a wide variety of sweet and savory dishes.
Green chilies (15) Green chilies are not indigenous to India but have become indispensable to Indian cuisine. They are very rich in vitamins A and C.
Gypsy beans (16) These have a slightly bitter taste but are delicious when cooked. Trim and string like any other bean before using.
Indian cheese (paneer) (17) Paneer is extremely popular in the north of India and is used in many vegetarian dishes for added nutrition. Long-life vacuum-packed paneer is available from Indian supermarkets and many health food stores.
Lemon (18) Lemons and limes are used to sour curries and make pickles and chutneys.

Mace (19) Mace is the dried covering of the nutmeg. It has a slightly bitter taste.
Mango (ripe) (20) Several varieties of mango are available but the best, 'alfonso', can only be found between May and July.
Mango (green) (21) Green mangoes are mainly used to make pickles and chutneys. They are sometimes added to south Indian curries.
Melon (22) Melon is often served in India for its cooling qualities.
Mint (23) Indian mint has a stronger aroma than the varieties available in the West.
Nutmeg (24) This aromatic and sweet spice is essential to many Indian dishes.
Okra (25) Okra is a very popular vegetable in India. It must be prepared and cooked with care to prevent the sticky insides from spreading among other ingredients in a dish.
Oranges (26) Oranges are refreshing served in wedges after a meal.
Pistachios (27) Pistachios are not indigenous to India and are therefore an expensive ingredient.
Purple beans (28) These beans have a broad, greenish purple pod with dark purple seeds. Trim and string before using.
Red chilies (29) Fresh red chilies vary in strength. The hottest are the smallest, known as 'bird's eyes'.
Red gram (30) Red gram is available dry or lightly oiled.
Red onion (31) Red onions are in fact a deep purple colour. They are more pungent than ordinary onions.
Santra (32) Santra is very refreshing after a curry meal. Serve wedges sprinkled with salt and pepper.
Spinach (33) India has over 15 varieties of spinach and it features in many vegetarian dishes.
Tamarind (34) Tamarind is a sour crescent-shaped fruit.
Tomato (35) The tomato is another ingredient introduced to India by the Portuguese, which now features in many dishes.
Vermicelli (36) These hair-like strands are made from wheat and are used in savory and sweet dishes. Indian is much finer than Italian vermicelli.
Walnuts (37) Walnuts are used in sweetmeats, salads, and raitha.

ONION FRITTERS

Bhajias

Bhajias are a classic snack of India. The same batter can be used with a variety of vegetables.

MAKES 20–25	1 tsp turmeric powder	2 large onions, finely sliced
	1 tsp baking powder	2 green chilies, finely chopped
Ingredients	1/4 tsp asafoetida	2oz cilantro leaves, chopped
8oz gram flour (besan), or channa atta	salt, to taste	cold water, to mix
1/2 tsp chili powder	1/2 tsp each, nigella, fennel, cumin, and onion seeds, coarsely crushed	vegetable oil, for deep-frying

1 In a bowl, mix together the flour, chili, turmeric, baking powder, asafoetida, and salt to taste. Pass through a strainer into a large mixing bowl.

2 Add the coarsely crushed seeds, onion, green chilies, and cilantro leaves, and toss together well. Very gradually mix in enough cold water to make a thick batter surrounding all the ingredients.

3 Heat enough oil in a karai or wok for deep-frying. Drop spoonfuls of the mixture into the hot oil and fry until they are golden brown. Leave enough space to turn the fritters. Drain well and serve hot.

YOGURT SOUP

Karhi

Some communities in India add sugar to this soup. When Bhajias are added, it is served as a main dish.

SERVES 4–6	1/2 tsp turmeric	3 cloves garlic, crushed
	salt, to taste	1 piece fresh ginger, 2in long, crushed
Ingredients	2–3 green chilies, finely chopped	3–4 curry leaves
1 1/2 cups plain yogurt, beaten	4 tbsp vegetable oil	fresh cilantro leaves, chopped, to garnish
4 tbsp gram flour (besan)	4 whole dried red chilies	
1/2 tsp chili powder	1 tsp cumin seeds	

1 Mix together the first 5 ingredients and pass through a strainer into a saucepan. Add the green chilies and cook gently for about 10 minutes, stirring occasionally. Be careful not to let the soup boil over.

2 Heat the oil in a frying pan and fry the remaining spices, garlic, and ginger until the dried chilies turn black.

3 Pour the oil and the spices over the yogurt soup, cover the pan, and leave to rest for 5 minutes off the heat. Mix well and gently reheat for 5 minutes more. Serve hot, garnished with the cilantro leaves.

LENTIL SOUP

Dhal Sherva

This is a simple, mildly spiced lentil soup, which is a good accompaniment to heavily spiced meat dishes.

SERVES 4–6

Ingredients
1 tbsp ghee
1 large onion, finely chopped
2 cloves garlic, crushed
1 green chili, chopped
½ tsp turmeric
3oz red lentils (masoor dhal)

1 cup water
salt, to taste
14oz canned tomatoes, chopped
½ tsp sugar
lemon juice, to taste
1 cup plain boiled rice or 2 potatoes, boiled
    (optional)
cilantro leaves, chopped, to garnish

1 Heat the ghee in a large saucepan and fry the onion, garlic, chili and turmeric until the onion is translucent.

2 Add the lentils and water and bring to a boil. Reduce the heat, cover, and cook until all the water is absorbed.

3 Mash the lentils with the back of a wooden spoon until you have a smooth paste. Add salt to taste and mix well.

4 Add the remaining ingredients. Reheat the soup and serve hot. To provide extra texture, fold in the plain boiled rice or potatoes cut into small cubes.

Cook's tip

When using lentils, first rinse in cold water and remove any floating items.

POTATO CAKES WITH STUFFING

Petis

Only a few communities in India make these unusual starters. Petis can also be served as a main meal with Tomato Salad.

MAKES 7–10

Ingredients

1 tbsp vegetable oil
1 large onion, finely chopped
2 cloves garlic, finely crushed
1 piece fresh ginger, 2in long, finely crushed

1 tsp ground coriander
1 tsp ground cumin
2 green chilies, finely chopped
2 tbsp each, chopped cilantro and mint leaves
8oz lean ground beef or lamb
2oz frozen peas, thawed
salt, to taste

juice of 1 lemon
2lb potatoes, boiled and mashed
2 eggs, beaten
bread crumbs, for coating
vegetable oil, for shallow-frying
lemon wedges, to serve

1 Heat the tbsp of oil and fry the first 7 ingredients until the onion is translucent. Add the meat and peas and fry well until the meat is cooked, then season with salt and lemon juice. The mixture should be very dry.

2 Divide the mashed potato into 8–10 portions, take a portion and flatten into a pancake in the palm of your hand. Place a spoonful of the meat in the center and gather the sides together to enclose the meat. Flatten it slightly to make a round shape.

3 Dip each petis in beaten egg and then coat in bread crumbs. Allow to chill in the refrigerator for about 1 hour.

4 Heat the oil in a frying pan and shallow-fry the cakes until all the sides are brown and crisp. Serve hot with lemon wedges.

SOUTH INDIAN PEPPER WATER

Tamatar Rasam

This is a highly soothing broth for winter evenings, also known as Pepper Water (Mulla-ga-tani). Serve with the whole spices or strain and reheat if you so wish. The lemon juice may be adjusted to taste, but this dish should be distinctly sour.

SERVES 4–6

Ingredients
2 tbsp vegetable oil
½ tsp freshly ground black pepper
1 tsp cumin seeds
½ tsp mustard seeds
¼ tsp asafoetida
2 whole dried red chilies
4–6 curry leaves
½ tsp turmeric
2 cloves garlic, crushed
1¼ cups tomato juice
juice of 2 lemons
½ cup water
salt, to taste
cilantro leaves, chopped, to garnish

1 In a large frying pan, heat the oil and fry the next 8 ingredients until the chilies are nearly black and the garlic golden brown.

2 Lower the heat and add the tomato juice, lemon juice, water, and salt. Bring to a boil, then simmer for 10 minutes. Garnish with the chopped cilantro and serve.

CHICKEN MULLIGATAWNY

Kozhi Mulla-ga-tani

Using the original Pepper Water – Mulla-ga-tani – this dish was created by the non-vegetarian chefs during the British Raj. The recipe was imported to the West via the United Kingdom and today ranks highly on many Indian restaurant menus as Mulligatawny soup.

SERVES 4–6

Ingredients
2lb chicken, boned, skinned and cubed
2½ cups water
6 green cardamom pods
1 piece cinnamon stick, 2in long
4–6 curry leaves
1 tbsp ground coriander
1 tsp ground cumin
½ tsp turmeric
3 cloves garlic, crushed
12 whole peppercorns
4 cloves
1 onion, finely chopped
4oz unsweetened cream of coconut
salt, to taste
juice of 2 lemons
deep-fried onions, to garnish
cilantro leaves, chopped, to garnish

1 Place the chicken in a large pan with the water and cook until the chicken is tender. Skim the surface, then strain, reserving the stock and keeping the chicken warm.

2 Return the stock to the pan and reheat. Add all the remaining ingredients, except the chicken, deep-fried onions, and cilantro. Simmer for 10–15 minutes, then strain and return the chicken to the soup. Reheat, garnish with deep-fried onions and chopped cilantro and serve.

PASTRY TRIANGLES WITH SPICY FILLING

Samosas

Traditional samosa pastry requires a lot of time and hard work but spring roll pastry makes an excellent substitute and is readily available. One packet will make 30 samosas. They can be frozen before or after frying.

MAKES 30	Filling	1 tsp amchur (dry mango powder)
Ingredients	3 large potatoes, boiled and coarsely mashed	1 small onion (red if available), finely chopped
1 packet spring roll pastry, thawed and wrapped in a damp towel	3oz frozen peas, boiled and drained	salt, to taste
vegetable oil, for deep-frying	2oz canned corn kernels, drained	2 green chilies, finely chopped
	1 tsp ground coriander	2 tbsp each, cilantro and mint leaves, chopped
	1 tsp ground cumin	juice of 1 lemon

1 Toss all the filling ingredients together in a large mixing bowl until well blended. Adjust seasoning of salt and lemon juice, if necessary.

2 Working with one strip of pastry at a time, place 1 tbsp of the filling mixture at one end of the strip and diagonally fold the pastry to form a triangle.

3 Heat enough oil for deep-frying and fry the samosas in small batches until they are golden brown. Serve hot with Fresh Cilantro Relish or a chili sauce.

SPICY OMELETE

Poro

Eggs are packed with nutritional value and make wholesome and delicious dishes. This omelete, cooked with potato, onion, and a touch of spices, can be put together quickly for an emergency meal.

SERVES 4–6
Ingredients
2 tbsp vegetable oil
1 medium onion, finely chopped
½ tsp ground cumin
1 clove garlic, finely crushed
1 or 2 green chilies, finely chopped
a few sprigs fresh cilantro, chopped
1 firm tomato, chopped
1 small potato, cubed and boiled
1oz cooked peas
1oz cooked corn kernels
salt and pepper, to taste
2 eggs, beaten
1oz grated cheese

1 Heat the oil in a saucepan and fry the next 9 ingredients until well blended but the potato and tomato are firm. Season to taste.

2 Increase the heat and pour in the beaten eggs. Reduce the heat, cover and cook until the bottom layer is brown. Turn the omelete over and sprinkle with the grated cheese. Place under a hot broiler and cook until the egg sets and the cheese has melted.

RICE LAYERED WITH CHICKEN AND POTATOES

Murgh Biryani

This dish is prepared mainly for important occasions, and is truly fit for royalty. Every cook in India has a subtle variation which is kept a closely-guarded secret.

SERVES 4–6

Ingredients

3lb boneless, skinless chicken breast, cut into large pieces
4 tbsp biryani masala paste
2 green chilies, chopped
1 tbsp crushed fresh ginger
1 tbsp crushed garlic
2oz cilantro leaves, chopped,
6–8 mint leaves, chopped, or 1 tsp mint sauce
⅔ cup plain yogurt, beaten
2 tbsp tomato paste

4 onions, finely sliced, deep-fried, and crushed
salt, to taste
1lb basmati rice, washed and drained
1 tsp black cumin seeds
1 piece cinnamon stick, 2in long
4 green cardamoms
2 black cardamoms
vegetable oil, for shallow-frying
4 large potatoes, peeled and quartered
¾ cup milk, mixed with ⅓ cup water
1 packet saffron powder, mixed with 6 tbsp milk
2 tbsp ghee or sweet butter

Garnish

ghee or sweet butter, for shallow-frying
2oz cashew nuts
2oz golden raisins
2 hard-cooked eggs, quartered
deep-fried onion slices, to garnish

1 Mix the chicken with the next 10 ingredients in a large bowl and allow to marinate for about 2 hours. Place in a large heavy pan and cook gently for about 10 minutes. Set aside.

2 Bring a large pan of water to a boil and soak the rice with the cumin seeds, cinnamon stick, and green and black cardamoms for 5 minutes. Drain well. Some of the whole spices may be removed at this stage.

3 Heat the oil for shallow-frying and fry the potatoes until they are evenly browned on all sides. Drain and set aside.

4 Place half the rice on top of the chicken in the pan in an even layer. Then make an even layer with the potatoes. Put the remaining rice on top of the potatoes and spread to make an even layer.

5 Sprinkle the water mixed with milk all over the rice. Poke random holes through the rice with the handle of a spoon and pour a little saffron milk into each hole. Place a few knobs of ghee or butter on the surface, cover, and cook over a low heat for 35–45 minutes.

6 While the biryani is cooking, make the garnish. Heat a little ghee or butter and fry the cashew nuts and golden raisins until they swell. Drain and set aside. When the biryani is ready, gently toss the rice, chicken, and potatoes together, garnish with the nut mixture, hard-cooked eggs, and onion slices and serve hot.

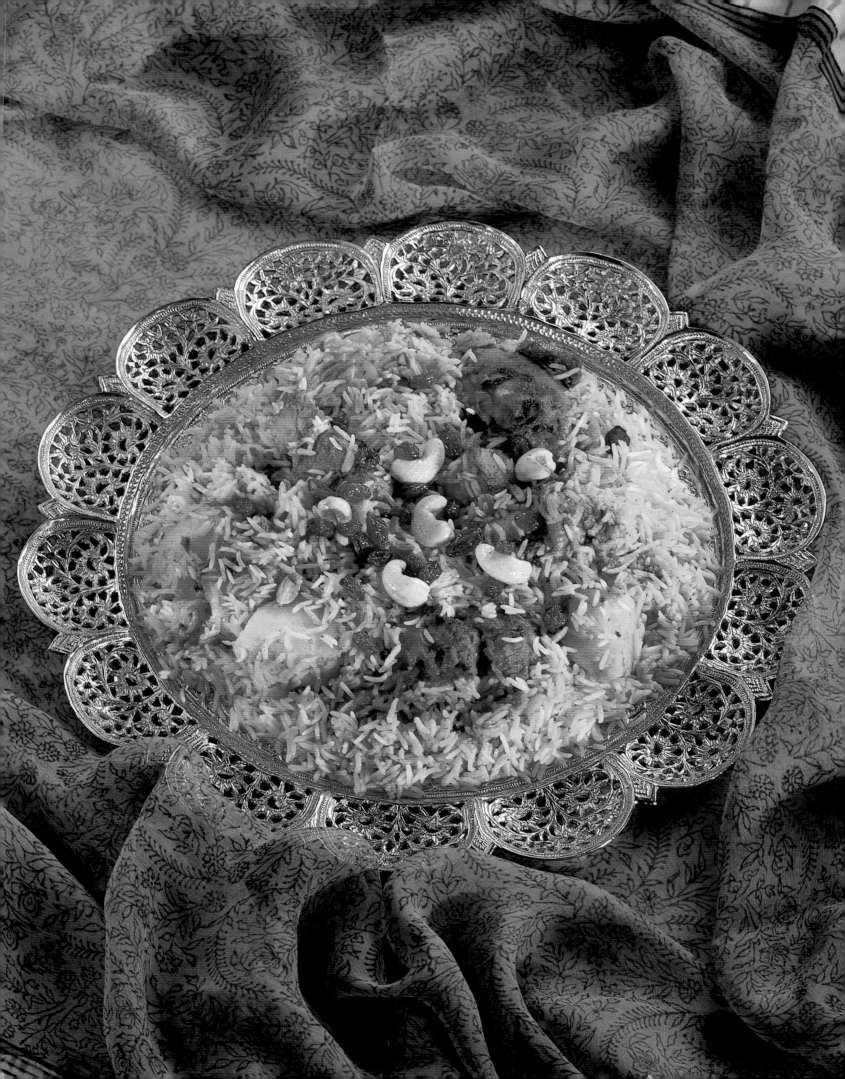

RICE LAYERED WITH SHRIMP

Jingha Gucci Biryani

This dish makes a meal in itself, requiring only pickles or raitha as an accompaniment. If serving for a party, complete your table with Boiled Egg Curry and Potatoes in a Red Hot Sauce.

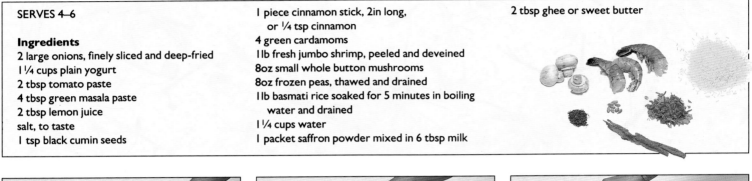

SERVES 4–6

Ingredients
2 large onions, finely sliced and deep-fried
1¼ cups plain yogurt
2 tbsp tomato paste
4 tbsp green masala paste
2 tbsp lemon juice
salt, to taste
1 tsp black cumin seeds

1 piece cinnamon stick, 2in long, or ¼ tsp cinnamon
4 green cardamoms
1lb fresh jumbo shrimp, peeled and deveined
8oz small whole button mushrooms
8oz frozen peas, thawed and drained
1lb basmati rice soaked for 5 minutes in boiling water and drained
1¼ cups water
1 packet saffron powder mixed in 6 tbsp milk

2 tbsp ghee or sweet butter

1 Mix the first 9 ingredients together in a large bowl. Fold the shrimp, mushrooms, and peas into the marinade and leave for about 2 hours.

2 Grease the base of a heavy pan and add the shrimp, vegetables and any marinade juices. Cover with the drained rice and smooth the surface gently until you have an even layer.

3 Pour the water all over the surface of the rice. Poke random holes through the rice with the handle of a spoon and pour a little saffron milk into each hole.

4 Place a few knobs of ghee or butter on the surface and place a circular piece of foil directly on top of the rice. Cover and cook over a low heat for 45–50 minutes. Gently toss the rice, shrimp, and vegetables together and serve hot.

Unleavened Bread Roasted with Ghee

Paratha

A richer, softer, and flakier variation on chappatis, parathas require longer preparation time so plan your menu well in advance. Like chappatis, parathas can be kept warm wrapped in foil.

MAKES 12–15

Ingredients
2⅔ cups atta (whole-wheat flour)
6 tbsp all-purpose flour
salt, to taste
6 tsp ghee
2 tsp ghee, melted

water, to mix
6 tbsp atta (whole-wheat flour), for dusting

1 Sift the flours and salt into a large mixing bowl. Make a well in the center and add 2 tsp of the ghee and fold into the flour to make a crumbly texture. Very gradually add enough water to make a soft but pliable dough. Cover and leave to rest for 1 hour.

2 Divide the dough into 12–15 equal portions and keep covered. Take one portion at a time and roll out on a lightly-floured surface to about 4in in diameter. Brush with a little of the melted ghee and sprinkle with atta. With a sharp knife, make a straight cut from the center to the edge.

3 Lift a cut edge and roll the dough into a cone shape. Lift it and flatten it again into a ball. Roll the dough again on a floured surface until it is 7in wide.

4 Heat a griddle and cook one paratha at a time, placing a little of the remaining ghee along the edges. Cook on each side until golden brown. Serve hot.

ROASTED UNLEAVENED BREAD

Chappati

Chappatis are prepared daily in most Indian homes. They are best eaten as soon as they are cooked although they can be kept warm, wrapped in foil and placed in a warm oven.

MAKES 10–12	1 tsp salt	ghee or sweet butter, for spreading
	water, to mix	
Ingredients	a few drops of vegetable oil, for brushing	
2⅔ cups atta (whole-wheat flour)	6 tbsp atta (whole-wheat flour), for dusting	

1 Sift the flour and salt into a large bowl. Make a well in the center and slowly add small quantities of water until you have a smooth but pliable dough. Grease the palms of your hands and knead the dough well. Keep covered until you are ready to use.

2 Divide the dough into 10–12 equal portions, using one portion at a time and keeping the rest covered. Knead each portion into a ball, then flatten with your hands and place on a floured surface. Roll out until you have a circle about 7in in diameter.

3 Heat a heavy griddle and, when hot, roast the chappatis on each side, pressing the edges down gently. When both sides are ready, brush the first side lightly with either ghee or butter.

LEAVENED BREAD

Naan

Traditionally, naans are baked in a tandoor or clay oven, though broiled naans look just as authentic.

MAKES 6–8	1lb all-purpose flour	1oz melted ghee or sweet butter
	1 tsp baking powder	flour, for dusting
Ingredients	½ tsp salt	ghee or sweet butter, for greasing
2 tsp active dry yeast	⅔ cup milk	chopped cilantro leaves and onion seeds, to
4 tbsp warm milk	⅔ cup plain yogurt, beaten	sprinkle
2 tsp sugar	1 egg, beaten	

1 Mix the yeast, warm milk, and sugar and leave to become frothy. Sift together the flour, baking powder, and salt. Make a well in the center and add the yeast mixture, milk, yogurt, egg, and ghee. Fold in all the ingredients.

2 Knead the dough well. Tightly cover the bowl and keep in a warm place until the dough doubles. To test, push a finger into the dough — it should spring back. Roll out the dough on a floured surface.

3 Make each naan slipper-shaped, about 10in long and about 6in wide, tapering to 2in. Sprinkle with the cilantro and onion seeds. Place on greased trays and then bake at 400°F.

Plain Boiled Rice

Chawal

In India, rice is consumed in great quantities by all members of society. There are numerous ways in which it can be prepared, but plain boiled rice is the most common.

SERVES 4–6	12oz basmati rice, washed and drained
	2 cups water
Ingredients	salt, to taste
1 tbsp ghee, sweet butter, or olive oil	

Cook's tip

To make Kesar Chawal or fragrant rice, sauté 4–6 green cardamoms, 4 cloves, 2in piece cinnamon stick, ½ tsp black cumin seeds, and 2 bay leaves. Add 12oz drained basmati rice and proceed as for plain boiled rice. For an even more luxurious rice, add 6–8 strands of saffron and sauté with the spices.

1 Heat the ghee, butter, or oil in a saucepan and sauté the drained rice thoroughly for about 2–3 minutes.

2 Add the water and salt and bring to a boil. Reduce the heat to low, cover, and cook gently for 15–20 minutes. To serve, fluff the grains gently with a fork.

Fragrant Rice with Meat

Yakhni Pilau

This rice dish acquires its delicious taste not only from the spices but the richly flavored meat stock.

SERVES 4–6	2 black cardamoms	8–10 saffron strands
	10 whole peppercorns	2 cloves garlic, crushed
Ingredients	4 cloves	1 piece fresh ginger, 2in long, crushed
2lb chicken pieces, or lean lamb, cubed	1 medium onion, sliced	1 piece cinnamon stick, 2in long
2½ cups water	salt, to taste	6oz golden raisins
4 green cardamoms	1lb basmati rice, washed and drained	sautéed blanched almonds, to garnish

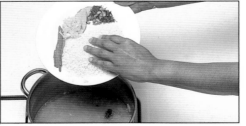

1 In a large saucepan, cook the chicken or lamb in the water with the cardamoms, peppercorns, cloves, onion, and salt until the meat is cooked. Remove the meat and keep warm. Strain the stock if you wish, and return to the saucepan.

2 Add the rice, saffron, garlic, ginger, and cinnamon to the stock and bring the contents to a boil.

3 Quickly add the meat and stir well. Bring back to a boil, reduce the heat, and cover. Cook, covered, for about 15–20 minutes. Remove from the heat for 5 minutes. Add the contents of the saucepan. Garnish with the raisins and almonds and serve.

RICE LAYERED WITH LENTILS AND GOURD CURRY

Dhal Chawal Palida

Bhori Muslims in India have their own special style of cooking and have adapted many of the traditional dishes from other Indian communities. Palida is prominently flavored with fenugreek and soured with kokum.(dried mangosteen). Lemon juice will provide the same effect.

SERVES 4–6

Ingredients
6oz bengal gram
2½ cups water
½ tsp turmeric powder
2oz deep-fried onions, crushed
3 tbsp green masala paste
a few mint and cilantro leaves, chopped
salt, to taste
12oz basmati rice, cooked
2 tbsp ghee or sweet butter

a little water
4 tbsp vegetable oil
¼ tsp fenugreek seeds
½oz dried fenugreek leaves
2 cloves garlic, crushed
1 tsp ground coriander
1 tsp cumin seeds
1 tsp chili powder
4 tbsp gram flour mixed with 4 tbsp water
1lb bottle gourd, peeled, pith and seeds removed, and cut into bite-size pieces (or use squash or firm zucchini)

¾ cup tomato juice
6 kokum (dried mangosteen), or juice of 3 lemons
salt, to taste
cilantro leaves, to garnish

1 For the rice, boil the bengal gram in the water with the turmeric until the grains are soft but not mushy. Drain and reserve the water for the curry.

2 Toss the bengal gram gently with the deep-fried onions, green masala paste, chopped mint and cilantro leaves, and salt.

3 Grease a heavy pan and place a layer of rice in the bottom. Add the bengal gram mixture and another layer of the remaining rice. Place small knobs of ghee on top, sprinkle with a little water, and gently heat until steam gathers in the pan.

---

4 To make the curry, heat the oil in a pan and fry the fenugreek seeds and leaves and garlic until the garlic turns golden brown.

5 Mix the spice powders to a paste with a little water. Add to the pan and simmer until all the water evaporates.

6 Add the remaining ingredients, and cook until the gourd is soft and transparent. Garnish with the cilantro leaves and serve hot with Dhal Chawal.

MOGHUL-STYLE ROAST LAMB

Shahi Raan

This superb dish is just one of many fine examples of the fabulous rich food once enjoyed by Moghul Emperors.
Try it as a variation to roast beef.

SERVES 4–6	2 tsp garam masala
	4–6 green chilies
Ingredients	juice of 1 lemon
4 large onions, chopped	salt, to taste
4 cloves garlic	1¼ cups plain yogurt, beaten
1 piece fresh ginger, 2in long, chopped	4lb leg of lamb
3 tbsp ground almonds	8–10 cloves
2 tsp ground cumin	4 firm tomatoes, halved and grilled, to serve
2 tsp ground coriander	1 tbsp blanched, slivered almonds, to garnish
2 tsp turmeric	

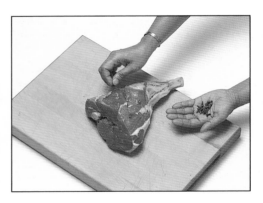

1 Place the first 11 ingredients in a food processor and blend to a smooth paste. Gradually add the yogurt and process until blended. Grease a large, deep baking tray and preheat the oven to 375°F.

2 Remove most of the fat and skin from the lamb. Using a sharp knife, make deep pockets above the bone at each side of the thick end. Make deep diagonal gashes on both sides.

3 Push the cloves into the meat at random.

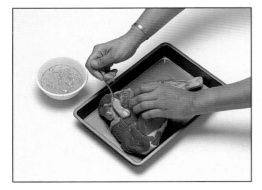

4 Push some of the spice mixture into the pockets and gashes and spread the remainder evenly all over the meat.

5 Place the meat on the baking tray and loosely cover the whole tray with foil. Roast for 2–2½ hours or until the meat is cooked, removing the foil for the last 10 minutes of cooking time.

6 Remove from the oven and allow to rest for 10 minutes before carving. Serve with grilled tomatoes and garnish the roast with slivered almonds.

KASHMIRI-STYLE LAMB

Rogan Josh

This curry originated in Kashmir, and derives its name from the large quantities of red chilies used in the dish. They can be reduced for a milder flavor, with paprika and 2 tsp tomato paste added to retain the color.

SERVES 4–6	2lb lean lamb, cubed	8–10 strands saffron (optional)
	1 piece fresh ginger, 2in long, crushed	salt, to taste
Ingredients	2 cloves garlic, crushed	2/3 cup plain yogurt, beaten
4 tbsp vegetable oil	4 tbsp rogan josh masala paste	slivered almonds, to garnish
1/4 tsp asafoetida	1 tsp chili powder or 2 tsp sweet paprika	

1 Heat the oil in a frying pan and fry the asafoetida and lamb, stirring well to sear the meat. Reduce the heat, cover, and cook for about 10 minutes.

2 Add the remaining ingredients except the yogurt and almonds and mix well. If the meat is too dry, add a very small quantity of boiling water. Cover and cook on a low heat for 10 minutes more.

3 Remove the pan from the heat and leave to cool a little. Add the yogurt, 1 tbsp at a time, stirring constantly to avoid curdling. Cook, uncovered, on low until the gravy becomes thick. Garnish and serve hot.

HOT DRY MEAT CURRY

Sookha Gosht

This dish is nearly as hot as phaal (India's hottest curry) but the spices can still be distinguished above the chili.

SERVES 4–6	4 cloves garlic, crushed	1 tsp turmeric
	6–8 curry leaves	salt, to taste
Ingredients	3 tbsp extra-hot curry paste, or 4 tbsp hot curry	2lb lean lamb, beef, or pork, cubed
2 tbsp vegetable oil	powder	3/4 cup thick coconut milk
1 large onion, finely sliced	3 tsp chili powder	2 large tomatoes, finely chopped, to garnish
1 piece fresh ginger, 2in long, crushed	1 tsp five-spice powder	

1 Heat the oil and fry the onion, ginger, garlic, and curry leaves until the onion is soft. Add the curry paste, chili, five-spice powder, turmeric, and salt.

2 Add the meat and stir well over a medium heat to sear and evenly brown the meat pieces. Keep stirring until the oil separates. Cover and cook for about 20 minutes.

3 Add the coconut milk, mix well, and simmer until the meat is cooked. Towards the end of cooking, uncover the pan to reduce the excess liquid. Garnish and serve hot.

Spicy Meat Loaf

Lagan Ki Seekh

This mixture is baked in the oven and provides a hearty breakfast on cold winter mornings.

SERVES 4–6	2 tbsp finely ground ginger	2oz cilantro leaves, chopped
	2 tbsp finely ground garlic	6oz potato, grated
Ingredients	6 green chilies, chopped	salt, to taste
5 eggs	2 small onions, finely chopped	
1lb lean ground beef	½ tsp turmeric	

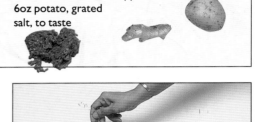

1 Preheat the oven to 350°F. Beat 2 eggs until fluffy and then pour into a greased loaf pan.

2 Knead the meat, ginger, and garlic, 4 green chilies, 1 chopped onion, 1 beaten egg, the turmeric, cilantro leaves, potato, and salt. Pack into the loaf pan and smooth the surface. Cook for 45 minutes.

3 Beat the remaining eggs and fold in the remaining green chilies and onion. Remove the baking tray from the oven and pour the mixture all over the meat. Return to the oven and cook until the eggs have set.

Spicy Kebobs

Kofta

Serve these tasty kebobs piping hot with Leavened Bread, Raitha, and Tomato Salad. Leftover kebobs can be coarsely chopped and packed into pita bread spread with Fresh Cilantro Relish.

MAKES 20–25	4 green chilies, finely chopped	4–6 mint leaves, chopped, or ½ tsp mint sauce
	1 small onion, finely chopped	6oz raw potato
Ingredients	1 egg	salt, to taste
1lb lean ground beef, or lamb	½ tsp turmeric	vegetable oil, for deep-frying
2 tbsp finely ground ginger	1 tsp garam masala	
2 tbsp finely ground garlic	2oz cilantro leaves, chopped	

1 Place the first 10 ingredients in a large bowl. Grate the potato into the bowl, and season with salt. Knead together to blend well and form a soft dough.

2 Shape the mixture into portions about the size of a golf ball. Leave to rest for about 25 minutes.

3 In a wok or frying pan, heat the oil to medium-hot and fry the koftas in small batches until they are golden brown in color. Drain well and serve hot.

LAMB KEBOBS

Shammi Kebab

Serve this Indian hamburger in a bun with chili sauce and salad or unaccompanied as an entrée.

SERVES 4–6

Ingredients
2 onions, finely chopped
9oz lean lamb, cut into small cubes
2oz bengal gram
1 tsp cumin seeds
1 tsp garam masala
4–6 green chilies
1 piece fresh ginger, 2in long, crushed
salt, to taste
¾ cup water
a few cilantro and mint leaves, chopped
juice of 1 lemon
1 tbsp gram flour
2 eggs, beaten
vegetable oil, for shallow-frying

1 Put the first 8 ingredients and the water into a pan and bring to a boil. Simmer, covered, until the meat and dhal are cooked. Cook, uncovered, to reduce the excess liquid. Cool, then grind to a paste.

2 Place the mixture in a mixing bowl and add the cilantro and mint leaves, lemon juice, and gram flour. Knead well. Divide into 10–12 portions and roll each into a ball, then flatten slightly. Chill for 1 hour. Dip the kebobs in the beaten egg and shallow-fry each side until golden brown. Serve hot.

CURRIED BEEF

Kheema

This can be served as a main dish or mixed with fried or scrambled eggs for a brunch. It also makes a good pizza topping.

SERVES 4–6

Ingredients
1 tsp vegetable oil
1 large onion, finely chopped
2 cloves garlic, crushed
1 piece fresh ginger, 2in long, crushed
4 green chilies, chopped
2 tbsp curry powder
1lb lean ground beef, or lamb
8oz frozen peas, thawed
salt, to taste
juice of 1 lemon
a few cilantro leaves, chopped

1 Fry the onion, garlic, ginger, and chilies until the onion is translucent. Lower the heat, add the curry powder, and mix well.

2 Add the meat and stir well, pressing the meat down with the back of a spoon. Add the peas, salt, and lemon juice. Mix well, cover, and simmer. Add the cilantro. Serve hot.

PORTUGUESE PORK

Soovar Vindaloo

This dish is a perfect example of the influence of Portuguese cooking on Indian cuisine.

SERVES 4–6

Ingredients
4oz deep-fried onions, crushed
4 red chilies, or 1 tsp chili powder
4 tbsp vindaloo masala paste
6 tbsp white-wine vinegar
6 tbsp tomato paste
½ tsp fenugreek seeds
1 tsp turmeric
1 tsp crushed mustard seeds, or ½ tsp mustard powder
salt, to taste
1½ tsp sugar
2lb boneless pork spareribs, cubed
1 cup water
plain boiled rice, to serve

1 Place all the ingredients except the water and rice in a heavy steel pan or mixing bowl and mix well. Marinate for 2 hours.

2 Add the water and mix well. Simmer gently for about 2 hours. Adjust the seasoning. Serve hot with the plain boiled rice.

STEAK AND KIDNEY WITH SPINACH

Sag Gosht

When this dish is cooked in India, the spinach is often pulverized. Here, it is chopped coarsely and added in the last stages of cooking, which retains the nutritional value of the spinach and gives the dish a lovely appearance.

SERVES 4–6

Ingredients
2 tbsp vegetable oil
1 large onion, finely chopped
1 piece fresh ginger, 2in long, crushed
4 cloves garlic, crushed
4 tbsp mild curry paste, or 4 tbsp mild curry powder
¼ tsp turmeric
salt, to taste
2lb sirloin and kidney, cubed
1lb fresh spinach, trimmed, washed, and chopped or 1lb frozen spinach, thawed and drained
4 tbsp tomato paste
2 large tomatoes, finely chopped

1 Heat the oil in a frying pan and fry the onion, ginger, and garlic until the onion is soft and the ginger and garlic turn brown.

2 Lower the heat and add the curry paste or powder, turmeric, salt, and meat and mix well. Cover the pan and cook until the meat is nearly tender.

3 Add the spinach and tomato paste and mix well. Cook, uncovered, until the spinach is softened and most of the liquid evaporated.

4 Fold in the chopped tomatoes. Increase the heat and cook for about 5 minutes.

MADRAS

Madras Attu Erachi

This popular south Indian curry is prepared mainly by Muslims and is traditionally made with beef.

SERVES 4–6	4 green cardamoms	1lb lean beef, cubed
	2 whole star anise	4 tbsp tamarind juice
Ingredients	4 green chilies, chopped	salt, to taste
4 tbsp vegetable oil	2 red chilies, chopped (fresh or dried)	sugar, to taste
1 large onion, finely sliced	3 tbsp madras masala paste	a few cilantro leaves, chopped, to garnish
3–4 cloves	1 tsp turmeric	

1 Heat the oil in a frying pan and fry the onion until it is golden brown. Lower the heat, add all the spice ingredients, and fry for a further 2–3 minutes.

2 Add the beef and mix well. Cover and cook on low heat until the beef is tender. Cook, uncovered, on a higher heat for the last few minutes to reduce any excess liquid.

3 Fold in the tamarind juice, salt, and sugar. Reheat the dish and serve hot, garnished with the chopped cilantro leaves.

LAMB IN A CREAMY SAUCE

Korma

This is a creamy, aromatic dish with no 'hot' taste. It comes from the kitchens of the Nizam of Hyderabad.

SERVES 4–6	6 cloves garlic, sliced	2lb lean lamb, cubed
	1 piece fresh ginger, 2in long, sliced	1 tsp ground cumin
Ingredients	1 onion, finely chopped	1 tsp ground coriander
1 tbsp white sesame seeds	3 tbsp ghee or vegetable oil	salt, to taste
1 tbsp white poppy seeds	6 green cardamoms	1¼ cups heavy cream mixed with ½ tsp
2oz blanched almonds	1 piece cinnamon stick, 2in long	cornstarch
2 green chilies, seeded	4 cloves	roasted sesame seeds, to garnish

1 Heat a frying pan without any liquid and dry-roast the first 7 ingredients. Cool the mixture and grind to a fine paste using a pestle and mortar or food processor. Heat the ghee or oil in a frying pan.

2 Fry the cardamom, cinnamon, and cloves until the cloves swell. Add the lamb, cumin, and coriander, and the prepared paste, and season. Cover and cook until the lamb is almost done.

3 Remove from the heat, cool a little, and fold in the cream, reserving 1 tsp to garnish. To serve, gently reheat the lamb, uncovered, and serve hot, garnished with the sesame seeds and the remaining cream.

POULTRY AND EGG DISHES

TANDOORI CHICKEN

Tandoori Murgh

This is probably the most famous of Indian dishes. Marinate the chicken well and cook in an extremely hot oven for a clay-oven-baked taste. If you want authentic 'charred' spots on the chicken, place the meat under a hot broiler for a few minutes after cooking.

SERVES 4–6

Ingredients
3lb ready-to-roast chicken
1 cup plain yogurt, beaten

4 tbsp tandoori masala paste
salt, to taste
3oz ghee or sweet butter
lettuce, to serve
lemon wedges and sliced onions, to garnish

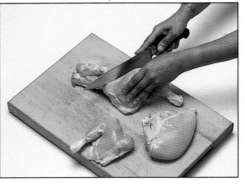

1 Using a sharp knife or scissors, carefully remove the skin from the chicken and trim off any excess fat. Using a fork, beat the flesh at random.

2 Cut the chicken in half down the center and through the breast. Cut each piece in half again. Make a few deep gashes diagonally into the flesh. Mix the yogurt with the masala paste and salt. Spread the chicken evenly with the yoghurt mixture, spreading some into the gashes. Leave for at least 2 hours, but preferably refrigerate overnight.

3 Place the chicken quarters on a wire rack in a deep baking tray. Spread the chicken with any excess marinade, reserve a little for basting halfway through cooking time.

4 Melt the ghee and pour over the chicken to seal the surface. This helps to keep the center moist during the roasting period. Cook in the oven for 10 minutes at maximum heat, then remove, leaving the oven on.

5 Baste the chicken pieces with the remaining marinade. Return to the oven and switch off the heat. Leave the chicken in the oven for about 15–20 minutes without opening the door. Serve on a bed of lettuce and garnish with the lemon and onion rings.

STUFFED ROAST CHICKEN

Murgh Mussallam

At one time, this dish was cooked only in royal palaces and ingredients varied according to individual chefs. The saffron and rich stuffing make it a truly royal dish.

SERVES 4–6

Ingredients
1 packet saffron powder
½ tsp ground nutmeg
1 tbsp warm milk
3lb whole chicken
6 tbsp ghee or sweet butter
⅓ cup hot water

Stuffing
3 medium onions, finely chopped
2 green chilies, chopped

2oz golden raisins
2oz ground almonds
2oz dried apricots, soaked until soft
3 hard-cooked eggs, coarsely chopped
salt, to taste

Masala
4 scallions, chopped
2 cloves garlic, crushed
1 tsp five-spice powder
4–6 green cardamoms
½ tsp turmeric
1 tsp freshly ground black pepper

2 tbsp plain yogurt
2oz toasted shredded coconut

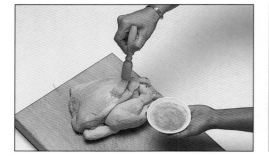

1 Mix together the saffron, nutmeg, and milk. Brush the inside of the chicken with the mixture and carefully spread some under the skin. Heat 4 tbsp of the ghee in a large frying pan or wok and fry the chicken on all sides to seal it. Remove and keep warm.

2 To make the stuffing, in the same ghee, fry the onions, chilies, and raisins for 2–3 minutes. Remove from the heat, allow to cool, and add the ground almonds, apricots, chopped eggs, and salt. Toss the mixture well, then stuff the chicken.

3 Heat the remaining ghee in a large heavy pan and gently fry all the masala ingredients, except the coconut, for 2–3 minutes. Add the water. Place the chicken on the bed of masala, cover the pan, and cook until the chicken is tender. Set aside and keep warm.

4 Return the pan to the heat and cook to reduce excess fluids in the masala. When the mixture thickens, pour over the chicken. Sprinkle with toasted coconut and serve hot.

CHICKEN CURRY

Murgh Ka Salan

Chicken curry is always popular whether served at a family dinner or banquet. This version is cooked covered, giving it a thin consistency. If you prefer it thick, cook uncovered for the last 15 minutes.

SERVES 4–6

Ingredients
4 tbsp vegetable oil
4 cloves
4–6 green cardamoms
1 piece cinnamon stick, 2in long
3 whole star anise
6–8 curry leaves
1 large onion, finely chopped
1 piece fresh ginger, 2in long, crushed
4 cloves garlic, crushed
4 tbsp mild curry paste
1 tsp turmeric
1 tsp five-spice powder
3lb chicken, skinned and cut in pieces
14oz canned tomatoes, chopped
4oz unsweetened cream of coconut
½ tsp sugar
salt, to taste
2oz cilantro leaves, chopped

1 Heat the oil in a frying pan and fry the cloves, cardamoms, cinnamon stick, star anise, and curry leaves until the cloves swell and the curry leaves are slightly burnt.

2 Add the onion, ginger, and garlic and fry until the onion turns brown. Add the curry paste, turmeric, and five-spice powder and fry until the oil separates.

3 Add the chicken pieces and mix well. When all the pieces are evenly seared, cover, and cook until the meat is nearly done.

4 Add the chopped tomatoes and the cream of coconut. Simmer gently until the coconut dissolves. Mix well and add the sugar and salt. Fold in the cilantro leaves, reheat thoroughly, and serve hot.

BOILED EGG CURRY

Andoan Ka Salan

This dish is usually served with biryani or pilau but it is equally good with Fried Whole Fish.

SERVES 4–6	1½ cups tomato juice	6 hard-cooked eggs, halved
	2 tsp gram flour (besan)	2 tbsp sesame oil
Ingredients	1 tsp finely crushed fresh ginger	1 tsp cumin seeds
2 tsp white poppy seeds	1 tsp chili powder	4 whole dried red chilies
2 tsp white sesame seeds	¼ tsp asafoetida	6–8 curry leaves
2 tsp whole coriander seeds	salt, to taste	4 cloves garlic, finely sliced
2 tbsp shredded coconut	1 tsp sugar	

1 Heat a frying pan and dry-fry the poppy, sesame, and coriander seeds for 3–4 minutes. Add the shredded coconut and dry-fry until it browns. Cool and grind the ingredients together using a pestle and mortar or a food processor.

2 Take a little of the tomato juice and mix with the gram flour (besan) to a smooth paste. Add the ginger, chili powder, asafoetida, salt, sugar, and the ground spices. Add the remaining tomato juice, place in a saucepan, and simmer gently for 10 minutes.

3 Add the hard-cooked eggs and cover with the gravy. Heat the oil in a frying pan and fry the remaining ingredients until the chilies turn dark brown. Pour the spices and oil over the egg curry, fold the ingredients together, and reheat. Serve hot.

EGGS BAKED ON SHOESTRING POTATOES

Sali Pur Eeda

Parsis love eggs, and have developed a variety of unique egg-based dishes such as this one.

SERVES 4–6	2 green chilies, finely chopped	⅓ cup water
	a few cilantro leaves, finely chopped	6 eggs
Ingredients	¼ tsp turmeric	salt and freshly ground black pepper, to taste
8oz shoestring potatoes	4 tbsp vegetable oil	3 scallions, finely chopped

1 In a bowl, mix the shoestring potatoes, chilies, cilantro, and turmeric. Heat 2 tbsp of the oil in a frying pan. Add the chipstick mixture and water. Cook until the chipsticks have softened, then fry until crisp.

2 Place a plate over the frying pan, turn the pan over, and remove the pancake onto it. Reheat the remaining oil in the pan and slide the pancake back to the frying pan to brown the other side.

3 Gently break the eggs over the pancake, cover the frying pan, and allow the eggs to set over a low heat. Season and sprinkle with the scallions. Cook until the base is crisp. Serve hot.

MOGHUL-STYLE CHICKEN

Moghlai Murgh

This delicate curry can be served as an entrée followed by stronger curries and rice. Saffron is crucial to the dish, but since it is very expensive, save this for special occasions.

SERVES 4–6

Ingredients
2 eggs, beaten with salt and pepper
4 chicken breasts, rubbed with a little garam
   masala
6 tbsp ghee or sweet butter
1 large onion, finely chopped
1 piece fresh ginger, 2in long, finely crushed
4 cloves garlic, finely crushed

4 cloves
4 green cardamoms
1 piece cinnamon stick, 2in long
2 bay leaves
15–20 strands of saffron
⅔ cup plain yogurt, beaten with 1 tsp cornstarch
salt, to taste
⅓ cup heavy cream
2oz ground almonds

1 Brush the chicken breasts with the beaten eggs. In a frying pan, heat the ghee and fry the chicken. Remove and keep warm.

2 In the same ghee, fry the onion, ginger, garlic, cloves, cardamoms, cinnamon, and bay leaves. When the onion turns golden, remove the pan from the heat, allow to cool a little, and add the saffron and yogurt. Mix well to prevent the yogurt from curdling.

3 Return the chicken mixture to the pan with any juices and cook gently until the chicken is tender. Adjust the seasoning if necessary.

4 Just before serving, fold in the cream and ground almonds. Serve hot.

CHICKEN IN A HOT RED SAUCE

Kashmiri Murgh

In India, small chickens are used for this dish and served as an individual starter with Unleavened Bread. If you wish to serve it as an entrée, use 4 Cornish game hens instead of chicken pieces. Skin them first and make small gashes with a sharp knife to enable the spices to seep in.

SERVES 4–6

Ingredients
4 tsp kashmiri masala paste
4 tbsp tomato ketchup
1 tsp Worcestershire sauce
1 tsp five-spice powder
salt, to taste

1 tsp sugar
8 skinless chicken pieces, with the bones
3 tbsp vegetable oil
1 piece fresh ginger, 2in long,
 finely shredded
4 cloves garlic, finely crushed
juice of 1 lemon
a few cilantro leaves, finely chopped

1 To make the marinade, mix together the kashmiri masala, tomato ketchup, Worcestershire sauce, five-spice powder, salt, and sugar. Allow to rest in a warm place until the sugar has dissolved.

2 Rub the chicken pieces with the marinade and allow to rest for 2 hours more, or refrigerate overnight if possible.

3 Heat the oil in a frying pan and fry half the ginger and all the garlic until golden brown. Add the chicken pieces, and fry without overlapping, until both sides are seared. Cover and cook until the chicken is nearly tender and the gravy clings with the oil separating.

4 Sprinkle the chicken with the lemon juice, remaining ginger, and cilantro leaves. Mix well, reheat, and serve hot.

CHICKEN IN SPICY ONIONS

Murgh Do Piyaza

This is one of the few dishes of India in which onions appear prominently. Chunky onion slices infused with toasted cumin seeds and shredded ginger add a delicious contrast to the flavor of the chicken.

SERVES 4–6

Ingredients
3lb chicken, cut in pieces and skinned
½ tsp turmeric
½ tsp chili powder
salt, to taste
4 tbsp oil

4 small onions, finely chopped
6oz cilantro leaves, coarsely chopped
1 piece fresh ginger, 2in long, finely shredded
2 green chilies, finely chopped
2 tsp cumin seeds, dry-roasted
⅓ cup plain yogurt
⅓ cup heavy cream
½ tsp cornstarch

1 Rub the chicken pieces with the turmeric, chili powder, and salt. Heat the oil in a frying pan and fry the chicken pieces without overlapping until both sides are seared. Remove and keep warm.

2 Reheat the oil and fry 3 of the chopped onions, 5oz of the cilantro leaves, half the ginger, the green chilies, and the cumin seeds until the onions are translucent. Return the chicken to the pan with any juices and mix well. Cover and cook gently for 15 minutes.

3 Remove the pan from the heat and allow to cool a little. Mix together the yogurt, cream, and cornstarch and gradually fold into the chicken, mixing well.

4 Return the pan to the heat and cook gently until the chicken is tender. Just before serving, stir in the reserved onion, cilantro, and ginger. Serve hot.

SPICY SWEET AND SOUR DUCK STEW

Dekchi Badak

This recipe can be made with any game bird, or even rabbit. It is a distinctively sweet-sour and hot dish, best eaten with rice as an accompaniment.

SERVES 4–6

Ingredients
3lb duck, cut in pieces and skinned
4 bay leaves
3 tbsp salt
¹⁄₃ cup vegetable oil
juice of 5 lemons

8 medium-sized onions, finely chopped
2oz garlic, crushed
2oz chili powder
1¼ cups distilled vinegar
4oz fresh ginger, finely sliced or shredded
½ cup sugar
2oz garam masala

1 Place the duck, bay leaves, and salt in a large pan and cover with cold water. Bring to a boil, then simmer until the duck is cooked through. Remove the pieces of duck and keep warm. Reserve the liquid as a base for stock or soups.

2 In a large pan, heat the oil and lemon juice until it reaches smoking point. Add the onions, garlic, and chili powder and fry the onions until they are golden brown.

3 Add the vinegar, ginger, and sugar and simmer until the sugar dissolves and the oil has separated from the masala.

4 Return the duck to the pan and add the garam masala. Mix well, then reheat until the masala clings to the pieces of duck and the gravy is thick. Adjust the seasoning if necessary. If you prefer a thinner gravy, add a little of the reserved stock.

SEAFOOD DISHES

BOMBAY DUCK PICKLE

Bomil Achar

This unusual fish is found off the west coast of India during the monsoon season. It is salted and dried in the sun and is characterized by a strong smell and distinctive piquancy. How this fish acquired the name Bombay Duck in the Western world still remains a mystery!

SERVES 4–6

Ingredients
6–8 pieces bomil (Bombay duck),
    soaked in water for 5 minutes
4 tbsp vegetable oil
2 fresh red chilies, crushed
1 tbsp sugar
1 lb cherry tomatoes, halved
4 oz deep-fried onions

1 Pat the soaked fish dry with paper towels. Heat the oil in a frying pan and fry the Bombay duck pieces for about 30–45 seconds on both sides until crisp. Be careful not to burn them as they will taste bitter. Drain well on paper towels. When cool, break the fish into small pieces.

2 In the same oil, cook the remaining ingredients until the tomatoes become pulpy and the onions are blended into a gravy. Fold in the Bombay duck pieces and serve hot or cold.

FISH CAKES

Macchli Kebabs

Kebobs are usually thought to be made with meat or chicken. These tasty fish kebobs can be made slightly larger and served as fish burgers, or made into small balls, and served on skewers as cocktail snacks.

MAKES 20

Ingredients
1 lb skinned haddock, coley, or cod
2 medium potatoes, peeled, boiled, and mashed

4 scallions, finely chopped
4 green chilies, finely chopped
1 piece fresh ginger, 2 in long, finely crushed
a few cilantro and mint leaves, chopped
salt and freshly ground black pepper, to taste

2 eggs
bread crumbs, for coating
vegetable oil, for shallow-frying
chili sauce or sweet chutney, to serve

1 Place the fish in a lightly greased steamer and steam until cooked. Remove but leave on the steaming tray to cool.

2 When the fish is cool, crumble it coarsely into a large bowl and mix in the potatoes, scallions, spices, cilantro, mint, seasonings, and 1 of the eggs.

3 Shape into cakes. Beat the remaining egg and dip the cakes in it, then coat with the bread crumbs. Heat the oil and fry the cakes until brown on all sides.

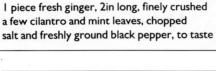

Shrimp and Fish in Herb Sauce

Haré Masalé Me Jingha Aur Macchi

Bengalis are famous for their seafood dishes and always use mustard oil in recipes because it imparts a unique taste and aroma. No Bengali feast is complete without one of these celebrated fish dishes.

SERVES 4–6

Ingredients
3 cloves garlic
1 piece fresh ginger, 2in long
1 large leek, roughly chopped
4 green chilies
1 tsp vegetable oil (optional)

4 tbsp mustard oil, or vegetable oil
1 tbsp ground coriander
½ tsp fennel seeds
1 tbsp crushed yellow mustard seeds, or 1 tsp mustard powder
¾ cup thick coconut milk
8oz firm fish, such as monkfish
8oz fresh jumbo shrimp, peeled and deveined, with tails intact
salt, to taste
4oz fresh cilantro leaves, chopped

1 In a food processor, grind the garlic, ginger, leek, and chilies to a coarse paste. Add vegetable oil if the mixture is too dry.

2 In a frying pan, heat the mustard or vegetable oil with the paste until it is well blended. Keep the window open and take care not to overheat the mixture as any smoke from the mustard oil will sting the eyes.

3 Add the ground coriander, fennel seeds, mustard, and coconut milk. Gently bring to a boil and then simmer, uncovered, for about 5 minutes.

4 Add the fish and simmer for 2 minutes then fold in the shrimp and cook until the shrimp turn a bright orange-pink color. Season with salt, fold in the cilantro leaves, and serve while hot.

PICKLED FISH STEAKS

Macchi Achar

This dish is served cold and makes a lovely entrée. It is also an ideal main course on a hot summer day served with a crisp salad. Make a day or two in advance to allow the flavors to blend.

SERVES 4–6		
Ingredients	4 thick fish steaks (any firm fish)	salt, to taste
juice of 4 lemons	4 tbsp vegetable oil	
1 piece fresh ginger, 1 in long, finely sliced	4–6 curry leaves	
2 cloves garlic, finely minced	1 onion, finely chopped	
2 fresh red chilies, finely chopped	½ tsp turmeric	
3 green chilies, finely chopped	1 tbsp ground coriander	
	½ cup distilled vinegar	
	3 tsp sugar	

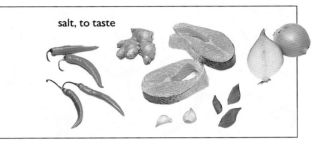

1 In a bowl, mix the lemon juice with the ginger, garlic, and chilies. Pat the fish dry with paper towels and rub the mixture on all sides of the fish. Allow to marinate for 3–4 hours in the refrigerator.

2 Heat the oil in a frying pan and fry the curry leaves, onion, turmeric, and coriander until the onion is translucent.

3 Place the fish steaks in the frying pan with the marinade and cover with the onion mixture. After 5 minutes, turn the fish over gently to prevent damaging the steaks.

4 Pour in the vinegar and add the sugar and salt. Bring to a boil, then lower the heat and simmer until the fish is cooked through. Carefully transfer the steaks to a large platter or individual serving dishes and pour over the vinegar mixture. Refrigerate for 24 hours before serving.

SHRIMP COOKED WITH OKRA

Jingha Aur Bhendi

This dish has a sweet taste with a strong chili flavor. It should be cooked fast to prevent the okra from breaking up and releasing its distinctive, sticky interior.

SERVES 4–6

Ingredients
4–6 tbsp oil
8oz okra, washed, dried, and left whole
4 cloves garlic, crushed

1 piece fresh ginger, 2in long, crushed
4–6 green chilies, cut diagonally
½ tsp turmeric
4–6 curry leaves
1 tsp cumin seeds
1lb fresh jumbo shrimp, peeled and deveined

salt, to taste
2 tsp brown sugar
juice of 2 lemons

1 Heat the oil in a frying pan and fry the okra on a moderately high heat until they are slightly crisp and browned on all sides. Remove them from the oil and set aside on paper towels.

2 In the same oil, gently fry the garlic, ginger, chilies, turmeric, curry leaves, and cumin seeds for 2–3 minutes. Add the shrimp and mix well. Cook until the shrimp are tender.

3 Add the salt, sugar, lemon juice, and fried okra. Increase the heat and fry quickly for 5 minutes more, stirring gently to prevent the okra from breaking. Adjust the seasoning, if necessary. Serve hot.

FRIED WHOLE FISH

Tali Huvey Macchi

In southern India, this fish dish is prepared daily in some form or another but most often it is just fried and served with a lentil curry and a hot pickle.

SERVES 4–6

Ingredients
1 small onion, coarsely chopped
4 cloves garlic, peeled
1 piece fresh ginger, 2in long, peeled
1 tsp turmeric
2 tsp chili powder
salt, to taste
4 red mullets
vegetable oil, for shallow-frying
1 tsp cumin seeds
3 green chilies, finely sliced
lemon or lime wedges, to serve

1 Using a food processor, grind the first 6 ingredients to a smooth paste. Make gashes on both sides of the fish and rub them with the paste. Leave to rest for 1 hour. Lightly pat the fish dry with paper towels without removing the paste. Excess fluid will be released as the salt dissolves.

2 Heat the oil in a large frying pan and fry the cumin seeds and chilies for about 1 minute. Add the fish and fry on one side without overlapping. When the first side is seared, turn the fish over very gently to ensure they do not break. Fry until they are golden brown on both sides, drain well, and serve hot with lemon or lime wedges.

STUFFED FISH

Bharey Huvey Macchi

Every community in India prepares stuffed fish but the Parsi version must rank top of the list. The most popular fish in India is the pomfret. These are available from Indian and Chinese grocers or large supermarkets.

SERVES 4–6

Ingredients
2 large pomfrets, or use Dover sole
2 tsp salt
juice of I lemon

Masala
8 tbsp shredded coconut
4oz fresh cilantro, including the tender stalks
8 green chilies (or to taste)

I tsp cumin seeds
6 cloves garlic
2 tsp sugar
2 tsp lemon juice

Cook's tip

In India, this fish dish is always steamed wrapped in banana leaves. Banana leaves are generally available from Indian or Chinese grocers but vine leaves from Greek food shops could be used instead.

1 Scale the fish and cut off the fins. Gut the fish and remove the heads, if desired. Using a sharp knife, make 2 diagonal gashes on each side, then pat dry with paper towels.

2 Rub the fish inside and out with salt and lemon juice and allow to stand for 1 hour. Pat dry thoroughly.

3 For the masala, grind all the ingredients together using a pestle and mortar or food processor, stuff the fish with the masala mixture, and rub any remaining into the gashes and all over the fish on both sides.

4 Place each fish on a separate piece of greased foil. Tightly wrap the foil over each fish. Place in a steamer and steam for 20 minutes or bake for 30 minutes at 400°F or until cooked through. Remove from the foil and serve hot.

PARSI SHRIMP CURRY

Kalmino Patio

This dish comes from the west coast of India, where fresh seafood is eaten in abundance. Fresh jumbo shrimp are really best for Patio and precooked or frozen will not give the same results.

SERVES 4–6

Ingredients
4 tbsp vegetable oil
1 medium onion, finely sliced
6 cloves garlic, finely crushed
1 tsp chili powder
1½ tsp turmeric
2 medium onions, finely chopped
¼ cup tamarind juice
1 tsp mint sauce
1 tbsp sugar
salt, to taste
1 lb fresh jumbo shrimp, peeled and deveined
3 oz cilantro leaves, chopped

1 Heat the oil in a frying pan and fry the sliced onion until golden brown. In a bowl, mix the garlic, chili powder, and turmeric with a little water to form a paste. Add to the onion and simmer for 3 minutes.

2 Add the chopped onions and fry until they become translucent, then fold in the tamarind juice, mint sauce, sugar, and salt. Simmer for 3 minutes more.

3 Pat the shrimp dry with paper towels. Add to the spice mixture with a small amount of water and stir-fry until the shrimp turn a bright orange-pink color.

4 When the shrimp are cooked, add the cilantro leaves and stir-fry on high heat for a few minutes to thicken the gravy. Serve hot.

HOT AND SOUR MEAT AND LENTIL CURRY

Dhansak

This is one of the best-known Parsi dishes and is a favorite for Sunday lunch. This dish has a hot, sweet and sour flavor, which should be permeated by the slightly bitter flavor of fenugreek.

SERVES 4–6

Ingredients
6 tbsp vegetable oil
5 green chilies, chopped
1 piece fresh ginger, 1 in long, crushed
3 cloves garlic, crushed
1 clove garlic, sliced
2 bay leaves
1 piece cinnamon stick, 2in long
2lb lean lamb, cut in large pieces
2½ cups water
6oz red gram
2oz each bengal gram, husked moong, and red lentils
2 potatoes, cut and soaked in water

1 eggplant, cut and soaked in water
4 onions, finely sliced, deep-fried, and drained
2oz fresh spinach, trimmed, washed, and chopped, or 2oz frozen spinach, thawed and drained
1oz fenugreek leaves, fresh or dried
4oz carrots (or pumpkin, if in season)
4oz fresh cilantro leaves, chopped
2oz fresh mint leaves, chopped, or 1 tbsp mint sauce
2 tbsp dhansak masala
2 tbsp sambhar masala
salt, to taste
2 tsp brown sugar
4 tbsp tamarind juice

Cook's tip

Chicken or shrimp can be used instead of the lamb. If using chicken, reduce the cooking time so that the meat does not become shredded or stringy; if you are using shrimp, cook only until the tails turn bright orange-pink in color.

1 Heat 3 tbsp of the oil in a saucepan or deep skillet and fry the green chilies, ginger, and crushed garlic cloves for 2 minutes. Add the bay leaves, cinnamon, lamb and water. Bring to a boil then simmer until the lamb is half cooked.

2 Drain the water into another pan and put the lamb aside. Add the lentils to the water and cook until they are tender. Mash the lentils with the back of a spoon.

3 Drain the eggplant and potatoes and add to the lentils with 3 of the deep-fried onions, the spinach, fenugreek, and carrot or pumpkin. Add some hot water if the mixture is too thick. Cook until the vegetables are tender, then mash again with a spoon, keeping the vegetables a little coarse.

4 Heat 1 tbsp of the oil and gently fry the cilantro and mint leaves (saving a little to garnish) with the dhansak and sambhar masala, salt, and sugar. Add the lamb and fry gently for about 5 minutes.

5 Return the lamb and spices to the lentil and vegetable mixture and stir well. As lentils absorb fluids, adjust the consistency if necessary. Then heat gently until the lamb is fully cooked.

6 Add the tamarind juice and mix well. Heat the remaining oil and fry the sliced clove of garlic until golden brown. Pour over the dhansak. Garnish with the remaining deep-fried onion and the reserved cilantro and mint leaves. Serve hot.

Lentils Seasoned with Fried Spices

Tarka Dhal

Dhal is cooked in every house in India in one form or another. This recipe is a simplified version.

SERVES 4–6

Ingredients
4oz red gram, washed and picked over
2oz bengal gram, washed and picked over
1½ cups water
4 whole green chilies

1 tsp turmeric
1 large onion, sliced
salt, to taste
14oz canned plum tomatoes, crushed
4 tbsp vegetable oil
½ tsp mustard seeds
½ tsp cumin seeds

1 clove garlic, crushed
6 curry leaves
2 whole dried red chilies
¼ tsp asafoetida
deep-fried onions and fresh cilantro leaves, to garnish

1 Place the first 6 ingredients in a heavy pan and bring to a boil. Simmer, covered, until the lentils are soft and the water has evaporated.

2 Mash the lentils with the back of a spoon. When nearly smooth, add the salt and tomatoes and mix well. If necessary, thin the mixture with hot water.

3 Fry the remaining ingredients until the garlic browns. Pour the oil and spices over the lentils and cover. After 5 minutes, mix well, garnish, and serve.

South Indian Lentils and Vegetables

Sambhar

This is a favorite south Indian dish served for breakfast with dosai (Indian pancake) or idli (rice dumplings).

SERVES 4–6

Ingredients
4 tbsp vegetable oil
½ tsp mustard seeds
½ tsp cumin seeds
2 whole dried red chilies
¼ tsp asafoetida

6–8 curry leaves
2 cloves garlic, crushed
2 tbsp shredded coconut
8oz red lentils picked, washed, and drained
2 tsp sambhar masala
½ tsp turmeric
1½ cups water
1lb mixed vegetables (okra, zucchini, cauliflower,

shallots, and bell peppers)
4 tbsp tamarind juice
4 firm tomatoes, quartered
4 tbsp vegetable oil
2 cloves garlic, finely sliced
a handful cilantro leaves, chopped

1 Fry the first 7 ingredients until the coconut browns. Mix in the lentils, sambhar masala, turmeric, and water.

2 Simmer until the lentils are mushy. Add the vegetables, tamarind juice, and tomatoes. Cook so the vegetables are crunchy.

3 Fry the garlic slices and cilantro leaves. Pour over the lentils and vegetables. Mix at the table before serving.

CURRIED CHICK PEAS WITH POTATO CAKES

Ragda Petis

No other city in India is quite like Bombay. Its cuisine is typical of food you can buy right off the streets, which is the way the Bombayites like it — spicy, quick, and nutritious.

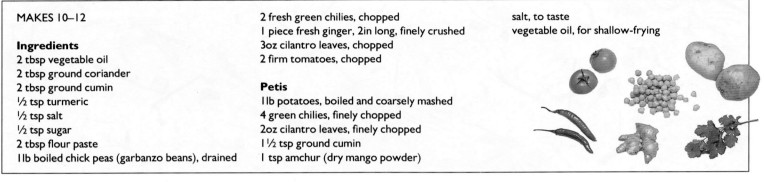

MAKES 10–12

Ingredients
2 tbsp vegetable oil
2 tbsp ground coriander
2 tbsp ground cumin
½ tsp turmeric
½ tsp salt
½ tsp sugar
2 tbsp flour paste
1lb boiled chick peas (garbanzo beans), drained

2 fresh green chilies, chopped
1 piece fresh ginger, 2in long, finely crushed
3oz cilantro leaves, chopped
2 firm tomatoes, chopped

Petis
1lb potatoes, boiled and coarsely mashed
4 green chilies, finely chopped
2oz cilantro leaves, finely chopped
1½ tsp ground cumin
1 tsp amchur (dry mango powder)

salt, to taste
vegetable oil, for shallow-frying

1 For the Ragda, heat the oil in a saucepan and fry the coriander, cumin, turmeric, salt, sugar, and flour paste until the water has evaporated and the oil separated.

2 Add the chick peas (garbanzo beans), chilies, ginger, cilantro leaves, and tomatoes. Toss well and simmer for 5 minutes. Transfer to a serving dish and keep warm.

3 To make the Petis, in a large mixing bowl mix the mashed potato with the green chilies, cilantro leaves, cumin, amchur powders, and salt. Mix until all the ingredients are well blended.

4 Using your hands, shape the Petis mixture into little cakes. Heat the oil in a shallow skillet or griddle and fry the cakes on both sides until golden brown. Transfer to a serving dish and serve with the Ragda.

BLACK GRAM IN A SPICY CREAM SAUCE

Masala Urad

Dhabas – highway cafes – are very lively eating places that serve a variety of dishes. This recipe is found almost everywhere and is one of the most popular.

SERVES 4–6

Ingredients
6oz black gram, soaked overnight
2oz red gram
½ cup heavy cream
½ plain yogurt
1 tsp cornstarch
3 tbsp ghee or sweet butter

1 onion, finely chopped
1 piece fresh ginger, 2in long, crushed
4 green chilies, chopped
1 tomato, chopped
½ tsp chili powder
½ tsp turmeric
½ tsp cumin powder
salt, to taste
2 cloves garlic, sliced

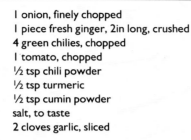

1 Drain the black gram and place in a heavy pan with the red gram. Cover with water and bring to a boil. Reduce the heat, cover the pan, and simmer until the gram are tender. The black gram will remain whole but the red gram will be mushy. Gently mash with a spoon. Allow to cool.

2 In a bowl, mix together the cream, yogurt, and cornstarch. Mix the cream mixture into the gram without damaging the whole black gram grains.

3 Heat 1 tbsp of the ghee in a frying pan and fry the onion, ginger, 2 of the green chilies, and the tomato until the onion is soft. Add the spices and salt and fry for 2 minutes more. Add it all to the gram mixture and mix well. Reheat and transfer to a heatproof serving dish and keep warm.

4 Heat the remaining ghee in a skillet and fry the garlic slices and remaining chilies until the garlic slices are golden brown. Pour over the gram and serve, folding the garlic and chili into the gram just before serving. Place extra cream on the table for the diners to add more if they wish.

BLACK-EYED BEANS AND POTATO CURRY

Lobia Aloo

Lobia are beige and kidney-shaped with a distinctive dark dot. This can be served as an entrée or snack.

SERVES 4–6

Ingredients
8oz lobia (black-eyed beans), soaked overnight
   and drained
¼ tsp bicarbonate of soda
1 tsp five-spice powder
¼ tsp asafoetida

2 onions, finely chopped
1 piece fresh ginger, 1in long, crushed
a few mint leaves
scant 2 cups water
4 tbsp vegetable oil
½ tsp each ground turmeric, coriander, and cumin
½ tsp chili powder
4 green chilies, chopped

⅓ cup tamarind juice
2 potatoes, peeled, cubed, and boiled
4oz cilantro leaves, chopped
2 firm tomatoes, chopped
salt, to taste

1 Place the lobia with the next 7 ingredients in a heavy pan. Simmer until the beans are soft. Remove any excess water and reserve.

2 Gently fry the spices, chilies, and tamarind juice until they are well blended. Pour over the lobia and mix.

3 Add the potatoes, cilantro leaves, tomatoes, and salt. Mix well, and if necessary add a little reserved water. Reheat and serve.

BENGAL GRAM AND BOTTLE GOURD CURRY

Doodhi Channa

This is an Anglo-Indian version of dhal, which is characteristically hot, and with the dhals left whole.

SERVES 4–6

Ingredients
6oz bengal gram, washed
scant 2 cups water
4 tbsp vegetable oil
2 green chilies, chopped

1 onion, chopped
2 cloves garlic, crushed
1 piece fresh ginger, 2in long, crushed
6–8 curry leaves
1 tsp chili powder
1 tsp turmeric
salt, to taste

1lb bottle gourd, zucchini, squash, or pumpkin,
   peeled, pithed and sliced
4 tbsp tamarind juice
2 tomatoes, chopped
a handful fresh cilantro leaves, chopped

1 In a saucepan, cook the lentils in the water until the grains are tender but not mushy. Put aside without draining away any excess water.

2 Fry the chilies, onion, garlic, ginger, curry leaves, chili powder, turmeric, and salt. Add the gourd pieces and mix. Cover and cook until the gourd is soft.

3 Add the lentils and water and bring to the boil. Add the tamarind juice, tomatoes, and cilantro. Simmer until the gourd is cooked. Serve hot, with a dry meat curry.

FLAVORED GREEN GRAM AND RICE

Kitchdee

The whole spices are edible, but it is advisable to warn the diners about them.

SERVES 4–6	1 piece ginger, 1 in long, shredded	salt, to taste
	4 green chilies, chopped	12oz patna rice, washed and soaked for
Ingredients	4 whole cloves	20 minutes
4 tbsp ghee	1 piece cinnamon stick, 1 in long	6oz split green gram, washed and soaked for
1 onion, finely chopped	4 whole green cardamoms	20 minutes
2 cloves garlic, crushed	1 tsp turmeric	2½ cups water

1 Gently heat the ghee in a large heavy pan with a tight-fitting cover and fry the onion, garlic, ginger, chilies, cloves, cinnamon, cardamoms, turmeric, and salt until the onion is soft and translucent.

2 Drain the rice and gram, add to the spices and sauté for 2–3 minutes. Add the water and bring to a boil. Reduce the heat, cover, and cook for about 20–25 minutes or until all the water is absorbed.

3 Take the pan off the heat and leave to rest for 5 minutes. Just before serving, gently toss the mixture with a flat spatula.

DRY MOONG DHAL WITH ZUCCHINI

Sookhi Moong Aur Chingri

Most dhal dishes are runny but this one provides textures with the addition of the lentils and the zucchini.

SERVES 4–6	1 large onion, finely sliced	6–8 curry leaves
	2 cloves garlic, crushed	salt, to taste
Ingredients	2 green chilies, chopped	½ tsp sugar
6oz moong dhal	½ tsp mustard seeds	7oz canned tomatoes, chopped
½ tsp turmeric	½ tsp cumin seeds	8oz zucchini, cut into small pieces
1¼ cups water	¼ tsp asafoetida	4 tbsp lemon juice
4 tbsp vegetable oil	a few cilantro and mint leaves, chopped	

1 In a saucepan, boil the moong dhal and turmeric in the water, then simmer until the dhal is cooked but not mushy. Drain and reserve both the liquid and the dhal.

2 Heat the oil in a frying pan and fry the remaining ingredients except the lemon juice. Cover and cook until the zucchini are nearly tender but still crunchy.

3 Fold in the drained dhal and the lemon juice. If the dish is too dry, add a small amount of the reserved water. Reheat and serve immediately.

BOMBAY POTATO

Bumbai Aloo

This authentic dish belongs to the Gujerati, a totally vegetarian sect and the largest population in Bombay.

SERVES 4–6	4 tbsp vegetable oil	¼ tsp asafoetida
	2 whole dried red chilies	½ tsp each, cumin, mustard, onion, fennel, and
Ingredients	6–8 curry leaves	nigella seeds
1lb whole new potatoes	2 onions, finely chopped	lemon juice, to taste
salt, to taste	2 green chilies, finely chopped	
1 tsp turmeric	2oz cilantro leaves, coarsely chopped	

1 Scrub the potatoes under running water and cut them into small pieces. Boil the potatoes in water with a little salt and ½ tsp of the turmeric until tender. Drain well, then mash coarsely. Set aside.

2 Heat the oil and fry the red chilies and curry leaves until the chilies are nearly burnt. Add the onions, green chilies, cilantro, remaining turmeric, and spice seeds and cook until the onions are soft.

3 Fold in the potatoes and add a few drops of water. Cook on low heat for about 10 minutes, mixing well to ensure the even distribution of the spices. Add lemon juice to taste, and serve.

CURRIED CAULIFLOWER AND PEAS

Phul Gobi Salan

In this dish the creamy, spiced coconut sauce disguises the strong smell of the spiced cauliflower.

SERVES 4–6	1 tbsp ground coriander	6–8 curry leaves
	1 tsp ground cumin	1 tsp cumin seeds
Ingredients	1 tsp mustard powder	1 cauliflower, broken into florets
1 tbsp gram flour	1 tsp turmeric	¾ cup thick coconut milk
½ cup water	salt, to taste	juice of 2 lemons
1 tsp chili powder	4 tbsp vegetable oil	

1 Mix the gram flour with a little of the water to make a smooth paste. Add the chili, coriander, cumin, mustard, turmeric, and salt. Add the remaining water and keep mixing to blend all the ingredients well.

2 Heat the oil in a skillet and fry the curry leaves and cumin seeds. Add the spice paste and simmer for about 5 minutes. If the gravy has become too thick, add a little hot water to thin.

3 Add the cauliflower and coconut milk. Bring to a boil, reduce the heat, cover, and cook until the cauliflower is tender but crunchy. Cook longer if you prefer. Add the lemon juice, mix well, and serve hot.

STUFFED OKRA

Bharé Huvey Bhendi

A delicious accompaniment to any dish, this can also be served on a bed of strained Greek yogurt which gives an excellent contrast in flavor.

SERVES 4–6

Ingredients
8oz large okra
1 tbsp amchur (dry mango powder)
½ tsp ground ginger
½ tsp ground cumin
½ tsp chili powder (optional)
½ tsp turmeric
salt, to taste
a few drops of vegetable oil
2 tbsp cornstarch, placed in a plastic bag
vegetable oil, for frying

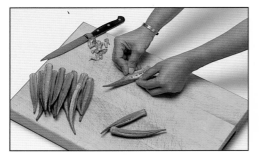

1 Wash the okra and dry on paper towels. Carefully trim off the tops without making a hole. Using a sharp knife, make a lengthwise slit in the center of each okra but do not cut all the way through.

2 In a bowl, mix the amchur, ginger, cumin, chili if using, turmeric, and salt with a few drops of oil. Leave the mixture to rest for 1–2 hours.

3 Using your fingers, part the slit of each okra carefully without opening it all the way and fill each with as much filling as possible. Put all the okra into the plastic bag with the cornstarch and shake the bag carefully to cover the okra evenly.

4 Fill a skillet with enough oil to sit 1in deep, heat it, and fry the okra in small batches for about 5–8 minutes or until they are brown and slightly crisp. Serve hot.

MIXED VEGETABLE CURRY

Sabzi Salan

This is a very delicately spiced vegetable dish that makes an appetizing snack when served with plain yogurt. It is also a good accompaniment to a main meal of heavily spiced curries.

SERVES 4–6

Ingredients
12oz mixed vegetables (beans, peas, potatoes, cauliflower, carrots, cabbage, eggplant, snow peas, and button mushrooms)
2 tbsp vegetable oil
1 tsp cumin seeds, freshly roasted
½ tsp mustard seeds
½ tsp onion seeds
1 tsp turmeric
2 cloves garlic, crushed
6–8 curry leaves
1 whole dried red chili
salt, to taste
1 tsp sugar
⅔ cup plain yogurt mixed with 1 tsp cornstarch

1 Prepare all the vegetables you have chosen: string the beans, thaw the peas, if frozen; cube the potatoes; cut the cauliflower into florets; dice the carrots; shred the cabbage; trim and string the snow peas; wash the mushrooms and leave whole.

2 Heat a large pan with enough water to cook all the vegetables and bring to the boil. First add the potatoes and carrots and cook until nearly tender, then add all the other vegetables and cook until still firm. All the vegetables should be crunchy except the potatoes. Drain well.

3 Heat the oil in a skillet and fry the spices gently until the garlic is golden brown and the chili nearly burnt. Reduce the heat.

4 Fold in the drained vegetables, add the sugar and salt, and gradually add the yogurt mixed with the cornstarch. Heat to serving temperature and serve immediately.

CURRIED SPINACH AND POTATO

Palak Aloo Sag

India is blessed with over 18 varieties of spinach. If you have access to an Indian or Chinese grocer, look out for some of the more unusual varieties.

SERVES 4–6

Ingredients
4 tbsp vegetable oil
8oz potato
1 piece fresh ginger, 1 in long, crushed
4 cloves garlic, crushed

1 onion, coarsely chopped
2 green chilies, chopped
2 whole dried red chilies, coarsely broken
1 tsp cumin seeds
salt, to taste
8oz fresh spinach, trimmed, washed, and chopped
   (or 8oz frozen spinach, thawed and drained)

2 firm tomatoes, coarsely chopped, to garnish

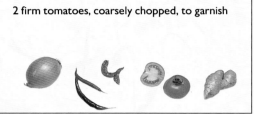

1 Wash the potatoes and cut into quarters. If using small new potatoes, leave them whole. Heat the oil in a skillet and fry the potatoes until brown on all sides. Remove and put aside.

2 Remove the excess oil leaving 1 tbsp in the pan. Fry the ginger, garlic, onion, green chilies, dried chilies, and cumin seeds until the onion is golden brown.

3 Add the potatoes and salt and stir well. Cook, covered, until the potatoes are tender when pierced with a sharp knife.

4 Add the spinach and stir well. Cook, uncovered, until the spinach is tender and all the excess fluids have evaporated. Garnish with the chopped tomatoes and serve hot.

CURRIED MUSHROOMS, PEAS, AND INDIAN CHEESE

Gucci Mattar Paneer

Paneer is a traditional cheese made from rich milk and is most popular with northern Indians. Rajasthani farmers eat this dish for lunch with thick parathas as they work in the fields.

SERVES 4–6

Ingredients
6 tbsp ghee or vegetable oil
8oz paneer, cubed
1 onion, finely chopped
a few mint leaves, chopped
2oz cilantro leaves, chopped
3 green chilies, chopped

3 cloves garlic
1 piece fresh ginger, 1 in long, sliced
1 tsp turmeric
1 tsp chili powder (optional)
1 tsp garam masala
salt, to taste
8oz tiny button mushrooms, washed and left
   whole
8oz frozen peas, thawed and drained

¾ cup plain yogurt, mixed with 1 tsp cornstarch
tomatoes and cilantro leaves, to garnish

1 Heat the ghee or oil in a skillet and fry the paneer cubes until they are golden on all sides. Remove and drain on paper towels.

2 Grind the onion, mint, cilantro, chilies, garlic, and ginger in a pestle and mortar or food processor to a fairly smooth paste. Remove and mix in the turmeric, chili powder if using, garam masala, and salt.

3 Remove excess ghee or oil from the pan leaving about 1 tbsp. Heat and fry the paste until the raw onion smell disappears and the oil separates.

4 Add the mushrooms, peas, and paneer. Mix well. Cool the mixture and gradually fold in the yogurt. Simmer for about 10 minutes. Garnish with tomatoes and coriander and cilantro and serve hot.

CORN-ON-THE-COB CURRY

Butta Salan

Corn-cobs are roasted on charcoal and rubbed with lemon juice, salt, and chili powder in India. In season, vendors fill the atmosphere with these delicious aromas. Corn is also a popular curry ingredient.

SERVES 4–6

Ingredients
4 whole corn cobs, fresh, canned, or frozen
vegetable oil, for frying
1 large onion, finely chopped
2 cloves garlic, crushed
1 piece fresh ginger, 2in long, crushed
½ tsp turmeric
½ tsp onion seeds
½ tsp cumin seeds
½ tsp five-spice powder
chili powder, to taste
6–8 curry leaves
½ tsp sugar
scant 1 cup plain yogurt

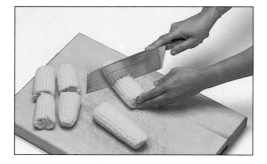

1 Cut each corn cob in half, using a sharp, heavy knife or cleaver to make clean cuts and prevent damaging the kernels. Heat the oil in a wok and fry the corn pieces until golden brown on all sides. Remove the corn cobs and set aside.

2 Remove any excess oil, leaving about 2 tbsp in the wok. Grind the onion, garlic, and ginger to a paste using a pestle and mortar or food processor. Remove and mix in all the spices, curry leaves, and sugar.

3 Heat the oil gently and fry the onion mixture until all the spices have blended well and the oil separates from the masala.

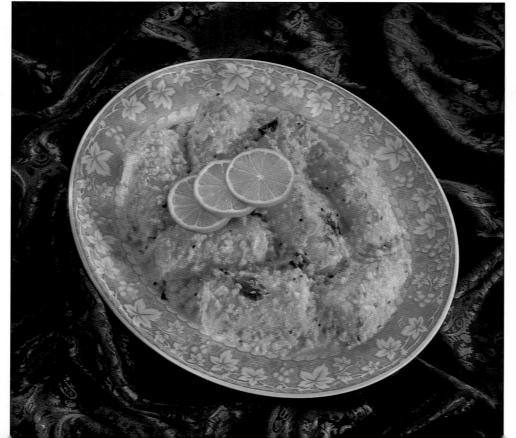

4 Cool the mixture and gradually fold in the yogurt. Mix well until you have a smooth sauce. Add the corn to the mixture and mix well so all the pieces are evenly covered with the gravy. Reheat gently for about 10 minutes. Serve hot.

CURRIED STUFFED BELL PEPPERS

Bharey Huvey Mirchi Ka Salan

This is one of the most famous dishes of Deccan. Hot, spicy and extremely delicious, it is often prepared for weddings. It is made with extra oil several days in advance to allow the spices to mature.

SERVES 4–6

Ingredients
1 tbsp sesame seeds
1 tbsp white poppy seeds
1 tsp coriander seeds
4 tbsp shredded coconut
½ onion, sliced
1 piece fresh ginger, 1 in long, sliced

4 cloves garlic, sliced
a handful of cilantro leaves
2 green chilies
4 tbsp vegetable oil
2 potatoes, boiled and coarsely mashed
salt, to taste
2 each, green, red and yellow bell peppers
2 tbsp sesame oil
1 tsp cumin seeds

4 green chilies, slit
4 tbsp tamarind juice

1 In a skillet, dry-fry the sesame, poppy, and coriander seeds, then add the shredded coconut and continue to roast until the coconut turns golden brown. Add the onion, ginger, garlic, cilantro, and chilies and roast for 5 minutes more. Cool, and grind to a paste using a pestle and mortar or food processor. Set to one side.

2 Heat 2 tbsp of the vegetable oil in a skillet and fry the ground paste for 4–5 minutes. Add the potatoes and salt and stir well until the spices have blended evenly into the potatoes.

3 Slice the tail ends off the bell peppers and reserve. Remove the seeds and any white pith. Fill the bell peppers with even amounts of the potato mixture and replace the tail ends on the top.

4 Heat the sesame oil and remaining vegetable oil in a skillet and fry the cumin seeds and the green chilies. When the chilies turn white, add the tamarind juice and bring to a boil. Place the bell peppers over the mixture, cover the pan, and cook until the peppers are nearly done.

POTATOES IN A HOT RED SAUCE

Lal Batata

This dish should be hot and sour but, if you wish, reduce the chilies and add extra tomato paste instead.

SERVES 4–6	4 cloves garlic	I tsp sugar
	6 tbsp vegetable oil	¼ tsp asafoetida
Ingredients	4 tbsp thick tamarind juice	cilantro leaves and lemon wedges, to garnish
I lb small new potatoes, washed and dried	2 tbsp tomato paste	
I oz whole dried red chilies, preferably kashmiri	4 curry leaves	
I ½ tsp cumin seeds	salt, to taste	

1 Boil the potatoes until they are fully cooked, ensuring they do not break. To test, insert a thin sharp knife into the potatoes. It should come out clean when the potatoes are fully cooked. Drain well.

2 Soak the chilies for 5 minutes in warm water. Drain and grind with the cumin seeds and garlic to a coarse paste using a pestle and mortar or food processor.

3 Fry the paste, tamarind juice, tomato paste, curry leaves, salt, sugar, and asafoetida until the oil separates. Add the potatoes. Reduce the heat, cover, and simmer for 5 minutes. Garnish and serve.

CUCUMBER CURRY

Kakri Ka Salan

This makes a pleasant accompaniment to fish dishes and can be served cold with cooked meats.

SERVES 4–6	salt, to taste	2 dried red chilies
	I tsp sugar	I tsp cumin seeds
Ingredients	I hothouse cucumber, cut into small pieces	I tsp mustard seeds
½ cup water	I large red bell pepper, cut into small pieces	4–6 curry leaves
4oz creamed coconut	2oz salted peanuts, coarsely crushed	4 cloves garlic, crushed
½ tsp turmeric	4 tbsp vegetable oil	a few whole salted peanuts, to garnish

1 Bring the water to a boil in a heavy pan and add the coconut, turmeric, salt, and sugar. Simmer until the coconut dissolves to obtain a smooth, thick sauce.

2 Add the cucumber, red bell pepper, and crushed peanuts and simmer for about 5 minutes. Transfer to a heatproof serving dish and keep warm.

3 Fry the chilies and cumin with the mustard seeds until they start to pop. Reduce the heat, add the curry leaves, garlic, and fry. Pour over the cucumber mixture and stir well. Garnish and serve hot.

HOT LIME PICKLE

Nimbu Achar

A good lime pickle is not only delicious served with any meal, it also increases the appetite and aids digestion.

MAKES 2 CUPS	8oz salt	½oz turmeric
	2oz ground fenugreek	2½ cups mustard oil
Ingredients	2oz mustard powder	I tsp asafoetida
25 limes	5oz chili powder	I oz yellow mustard seeds, crushed

1 Cut each lime into 8 pieces and remove the seeds, if you wish. Place the limes in a large sterilized jar or glass bowl. Add the salt and toss with the limes. Cover and leave in a warm place until they become soft and dull brown in color, for 1 to 2 weeks.

2 Mix together the fenugreek, mustard powder, chili powder, and turmeric and add to the limes. Cover and leave to rest in a warm place for 2 or 3 days more.

3 Heat the mustard oil in a skillet and fry the asafoetida and mustard seeds. When the oil reaches smoking point, pour it over the limes. Mix well, cover with a clean cloth, and then leave in a warm place for about 1 week before serving.

GREEN CHILI PICKLE

Mirchi Ka Achar

Southern India is the source of some of the hottest curries and pickles, which are said to cool the body.

MAKES 2–2½ CUPS	I oz turmeric	⅔ cup mustard oil
	2oz garlic cloves, crushed	20 small garlic cloves, peeled and left whole
Ingredients	⅔ cup distilled white vinegar	I lb small green chilies, washed, dried, and halved
2oz yellow mustard seeds, crushed	3oz sugar	
2oz freshly ground cumin seeds	2 tsp salt	

1 Mix the mustard seeds, cumin, turmeric, crushed garlic, vinegar, sugar, and salt together in a sterilized glass bowl. Cover with a cloth and allow to rest for 24 hours. This enables the spices to infuse and the sugar and salt to dissolve.

2 Heat the mustard oil and gently fry the spice mixture for about 5 minutes. (Keep a window open while cooking with mustard oil as it is pungent and the smoke may irritate the eyes.) Add the garlic cloves and fry for 5 minutes more.

3 Add the chilies and cook gently until tender but still green in color. This will take about 30 minutes on a low heat. Cool thoroughly and pour into sterilized bottles, ensuring the oil is evenly distributed if you are using more than one bottle. Leave to rest for 1 week before serving.

SPICED YOGURT

Tarka Dahi

Yogurt is always a welcome accompaniment to hot curries. This has been given a final fry with spices just to flavor the yogurt slightly.

MAKES 2 CUPS

Ingredients
scant 2 cups plain yogurt
½ tsp freshly ground fennel seeds
salt, to taste
½ tsp sugar
4 tbsp vegetable oil
1 whole dried red chili
¼ tsp mustard seeds
¼ tsp cumin seeds
4–6 curry leaves
a pinch each of asafoetida and turmeric

1 In a heatproof serving dish, mix together the yogurt, fennel seeds, salt, and sugar and chill until you are nearly ready to serve.

2 Heat the oil in a skillet and fry the chili, mustard and cumin seeds, curry leaves, asafoetida, and turmeric. When the chili turns dark, pour the oil and spices over the yogurt. Fold the yogurt together with the spices at the table before serving.

YOGURT SALAD

Mava Raitha

Raithas are served to cool the effect of hot curries. Cucumber and mint raitha is most commonly served, so why not try a variation?

SERVES 4

Ingredients
1½ cups plain yogurt
3oz seedless grapes, washed and dried
2oz shelled walnuts
2 firm bananas
1 tsp sugar
salt, to taste
1 tsp freshly ground cumin seeds
¼ tsp freshly roasted cumin seeds,
chili powder, or paprika, to garnish

1 Place the yogurt in a chilled bowl and add the grapes and walnuts. Slice the bananas directly into the bowl and fold in gently before the bananas turn brown.

2 Add the sugar, salt, and ground cumin, and gently mix together. Chill, and just before serving, sprinkle on the cumin seeds, chili powder, or paprika.

TOMATO SALAD

Tamatar Kasondi

This is a simple relish served with most meals. It provides a contrast to hot curries, with its crunchy texture and refreshing ingredients.

SERVES 4–6

Ingredients
2 limes
½ tsp sugar
salt and freshly ground black pepper, to taste
2 onions, finely chopped
4 firm tomatoes, finely chopped
½ cucumber, finely chopped
1 green chili, finely chopped
a few cilantro leaves, chopped
a few mint leaves, to garnish

1 Extract the juice of the limes into a small bowl and add the sugar, salt, and pepper. Allow to rest until the sugar and salt have dissolved. Mix together well.

2 Add the onions, tomatoes, cucumber, chili and cilantro leaves, reserving a few. Chill, and garnish with cilantro and mint before serving.

FRESH CILANTRO RELISH

Hara Dhaniya Chutney

Delicious as an accompaniment to kebobs, samosas, and bhajias, this relish can also be used as a spread for cucumber or tomato sandwiches.

MAKES 1¾ CUPS

Ingredients
2 tbsp vegetable oil
1 dried red chili
¼ tsp each, cumin, fennel, and onion seeds
¼ tsp asafoetida
4 curry leaves
4oz shredded coconut
2 tsp sugar
salt, to taste
3 green chilies
6–8oz cilantro leaves
4 tbsp mint sauce
juice of 3 lemons

1 Fry the red chili, cumin, fennel and onion seeds, asafoetida, curry leaves, shredded coconut, sugar, and salt until the coconut turns golden brown. Cool.

2 Grind the spice mixture with the green chilies, cilantro leaves, and mint sauce. Moisten with lemon juice. Remove, and chill before serving.

TOMATO CHUTNEY

Kachoomber

This delicious relish is especially suited to lentil dishes. If kept refrigerated, it can be made a week before serving.

MAKES 2–2¼ CUPS

Ingredients
6 tbsp vegetable oil
1 piece cinnamon stick, 2in long
4 cloves
1 tsp freshly roasted cumin seeds
1 tsp nigella seeds
4 bay leaves
1 tsp mustard seeds, crushed
4 cloves garlic, crushed
1 piece fresh ginger, 2in long, crushed
1 tsp chili powder
1 tsp turmeric
4 tbsp brown sugar
1¾ lb canned, chopped tomatoes, drained (reserving juices)

1 Heat the oil on a medium heat and fry the cinnamon, cloves, cumin and nigella seeds, bay leaves, and mustard seeds for about 5 minutes. Add the garlic and fry until golden brown.

2 Add the ginger, chili powder, turmeric, sugar, and the reserved tomato juices. Simmer until reduced, add the tomatoes, and cook for 15–20 minutes. Cool and serve.

MANGO CHUTNEY

Kairi Ki Chutni

Chutneys are usually served as an accompaniment to curry but this one is particularly nice served in a cheese sandwich or as a dip with papadums.

MAKES 2 CUPS

Ingredients
¼ cup malt vinegar
½ tsp dried chilies, crushed
6 whole cloves
6 whole peppercorns
1 tsp roasted cumin seeds
½ tsp onion seeds
salt, to taste
6oz sugar
1lb unripe mango, peeled and cubed
1 piece fresh ginger, 2in long, finely sliced
2 cloves garlic, crushed
thin peel of 1 orange or lemon (optional)

1 In a saucepan, heat the vinegar with the chilies, cloves, peppercorns, cumin and onion seeds, salt, and sugar. Simmer until the flavors of the spices infuse into the vinegar — about 15 minutes on low heat.

2 Add the mango, ginger, garlic, and peel, if using. Simmer until the mango is mushy and most of the vinegar has evaporated. When cool, pour into sterilized bottles. Leave for a few days before serving.

AVOCADO SALAD

Makhan Chaat

In India, avocados are called butter fruit, reflecting their subtle taste. This delicate dish makes a good entrée.

SERVES 4–6	4oz cottage cheese with chives	a few lettuce leaves, shredded (a mixed variety
	1 clove garlic, crushed	makes a good display)
Ingredients	2 green chilies, finely chopped	paprika and mint leaves, to garnish
2 avocados	salt and pepper, to taste	
⅓ cup plain yogurt, beaten	a little lemon juice	

1 Halve the avocados and remove the pits. Gently scoop out the flesh, reserving the skins, and cut into small cubes. In a bowl, mix the yogurt, cottage cheese, garlic, chilies, and salt and pepper, and fold in the avocado cubes. Chill in the refrigerator.

2 Rub the avocado skins with some lemon juice and line each cavity with some shredded lettuce. Top with the chilled mixture, garnish with the paprika and mint leaves, and serve immediately.

INDIAN FRUIT SALAD

Phul Chaat

This is a very appetizing and refreshing salad, with a typically Indian combination of citrus fruits seasoned with salt and pepper. It will provide the perfect ending to a heavy meal.

SERVES 6	2 navel oranges, peeled and segmented	juice of 1 lemon
	8oz canned grapefruit segments, drained	salt and freshly ground black pepper, to taste
Ingredients	balls from 1 honeydew melon	½ tsp sugar
4oz seedless green and black grapes	balls from ½ watermelon (when in season)	¼ tsp freshly ground cumin seeds
8oz canned mandarin segments, drained	1 fresh mango, peeled and sliced	

1 Place all the fruit in a large serving bowl and add the lemon juice. Gently toss to prevent damaging the fruit.

2 Mix together the remaining ingredients and sprinkle over the fruit. Gently toss, chill thoroughly, and serve.

RICE PUDDING

Kheer

Both Muslim and Hindu communities prepare this sweet, which is traditionally served at mosques and temples.

SERVES 4–6	1 piece cinnamon stick, 2in long	1 tsp ground cardamom
	1 1/3 cups soft brown sugar	2oz golden raisins
Ingredients	4oz coarsely ground rice	1oz slivered almonds
1 tbsp ghee or sweet butter	5 cups whole milk	1/2 tsp freshly ground nutmeg, to serve

1 In a heavy pan, melt the ghee and fry the cinnamon and sugar. Keep frying until the sugar begins to caramelize. Reduce the heat immediately when this happens.

2 Add the rice and half of the milk. Bring to a boil, stirring constantly to avoid the milk boiling over. Reduce the heat and simmer until the rice is cooked, stirring regularly.

3 Add the remaining milk, cardamom, raisins, and almonds and leave to simmer, but keep stirring to prevent the kheer from sticking to the base of the pan. When the mixture has thickened, serve hot or cold, sprinkled with the nutmeg.

VERMICELLI PUDDING

Shirkhuma

This sweet is prepared by Muslims very early in the morning of Id-ul-Fitr, the feast after the 30 days of Ramadan.

SERVES 4–6	1oz slivered almonds	4 cups whole milk
	1oz pistachios, slivered	4 tbsp dark brown sugar
Ingredients	1oz cudapah nuts	1 packet saffron powder
6 tbsp ghee or sweet butter	2oz golden raisins	
4oz vermicelli, coarsely broken	2oz dates, pitted and slivered	

1 Heat 4 tbsp of the ghee in a skillet and sauté the vermicelli until golden brown. (If you are using the Italian variety, sauté it a little longer.) Remove and set aside.

2 Heat the remaining ghee and fry the nuts, raisins, and dates until the raisins swell. Add to the vermicelli.

3 Heat the milk in a large heavy pan and add the sugar. Bring to a boil, add the vermicelli mixture, and boil, stirring constantly. Reduce the heat and simmer until the vermicelli is soft and you have a fairly thick pudding. Fold in the saffron powder and serve hot or cold.

INDIAN ICE CREAM

Kulfi

Kulfi-wallahs (ice cream vendors) have always made kulfi, and continue to this day, without using modern freezers. Kulfi is packed into metal cones sealed with dough and then churned in clay pots until set. Try this method – it works extremely well in an ordinary freezer.

SERVES 4–6

Ingredients
3 × 14oz cans evaporated milk
3 egg whites, whisked until peaks form
1⅓ cups confectioners' sugar

1 tsp ground cardamom
1 tbsp rose water
6oz pistachios, chopped
3oz golden raisins
3oz sliced almonds
1oz candied cherries, halved

1 Remove the labels from the cans of evaporated milk and lay the cans down in a pan with a tight-fitting lid. Fill the pan with water to reach three-quarters up the cans. Bring to a boil, cover, and simmer for 20 minutes. When cool, remove and chill the cans in the refrigerator for 24 hours.

2 Open the cans and empty the milk into a large, chilled bowl. Whisk until it doubles in quantity, then fold in the whisked egg whites and confectioners' sugar.

3 Gently fold in the remaining ingredients, seal the bowl with plastic wrap and leave in the freezer for 1 hour.

4 Remove the ice cream from the freezer and mix well with a fork. Transfer to a serving container and return to the freezer for a final setting. Remove from the freezer 10 minutes before serving.

MANGO SHERBET WITH SAUCE

Baraf Ke Aamb

After a heavy meal, this makes a very refreshing dessert. Mango is said to be one of the oldest fruits cultivated in India, having been brought by Lord Shiva for his beautiful wife, Parvathi.

SERVES 4–6

Ingredients
2lb mango pulp
½ tsp lemon juice

peel of 1 orange and 1 lemon, grated
4 egg whites, whisked until peaks form
6 tbsp superfine sugar
½ cup heavy cream
2oz confectioners' sugar

1 In a large, chilled bowl, mix 15oz of the mango pulp together with the lemon juice and the peel.

2 Gently fold in the egg whites and super-fine sugar. Cover with plastic wrap and place in the freezer for at least 1 hour.

3 Remove and beat again. Transfer to an ice cream container and freeze until fully set.

4 Whip the heavy cream with the confec-tioners' sugar and the remaining mango pulp. Chill the sauce for 24 hours. Remove the sherbet 10 minutes before serving. Scoop out individual servings and cover with a generous helping of mango sauce. Serve immediately.

TEA AND FRUIT PUNCH

Chai Sherbet

This delicious punch may be served hot or cold. White wine or brandy may be added to taste.

MAKES 3½ CUPS

Ingredients
2½ cups water
I cinnamon stick

4 cloves
2½ tsp Earl Grey tea leaves
6oz sugar
1½ cups tropical soft drink concentrate
I lemon, sliced

I small orange, sliced
½ hothouse cucumber, sliced

1 Bring the water to a boil in a saucepan with the cinnamon and cloves. Remove from the heat and add the tea leaves and allow to brew for 5 minutes. Stir and strain into a large chilled bowl.

2 Add the sugar and the soft drink concentrate and allow to rest until the sugar has dissolved and the mixture cooled. Place the fruit and cucumber in a chilled punch bowl and pour over the tea mix. Chill for 24 hours before serving.

BUTTERMILK

Lassi

Buttermilk is prepared by churning yogurt with water and then removing the fat. To make this refreshing drink without churning, use low-fat plain yogurt.

SERVES 4

Ingredients
1½ cups plain yogurt

1¼ cups water
I piece fresh ginger, I in long, finely crushed
2 green chilies, finely chopped
½ tsp ground cumin

salt and freshly ground black pepper, to taste
a few cilantro leaves, chopped, to garnish

1 In a bowl, whisk the yogurt and water until well blended. The consistency should be that of whole milk. Adjust by adding more water if necessary.

2 Add the ginger, chilies, and ground cumin, season with the salt and pepper, and mix well. Divide into 4 serving glasses and chill. Garnish with cilantro before serving.

Cook's tip

To make sweet lassi, mix the yogurt and water together with 6 tbsp sugar, 1 tsp freshly ground cumin powder, ½ tsp ground cardamom and a pinch of salt and pepper. Whisk all the ingredients together, chill, and serve.

ACKNOWLEDGEMENTS

The authors and publishers would like to thank the following for generously supplying food products and equipment:

B E International Foods Limited
Grafton House
Stockingwater Lane
Enfield
Middlesex EN3

Cherry Valley Farms Ltd
Rotherwell, Lincoln

Wing Yip
395 Edgware Road
London NW2

The authors and publishers would like to thank the following for their invaluable advice and assistance:

Mrs Duc Cung; Shobana Jeyasingh; Jane Wheeler; Yum Yum Restaurant, London N16

STOCKISTS AND SUPPLIERS

United States
Chinese food and equipment

Arizona
G&L Import-Export Corp. 4828 East 22nd Street, Tuscon, Arizona, 85706, (602) 790-9016

California
Chinese Grocer 209 Post Street, San Francisco, California, 94108, (415) 982-0125

Good Earth Seed Co. P.O. Box 5644, Redwood City, California, 94603, (415) 595-2270

Illinois
Bangkok Oriental Grocery 7430 Harlem Avenue, Bridgeview, Illinois 60455, (708) 458-1810

Chang Oriental Foods 5214 North Lincoln Avenue, Chicago, Illinois, 60646, (312) 271-5050

Massachusetts
Chung Wah Hong Co. 55 Beach Street, Boston, Massachusetts, 02111, (617) 426-3619

See Sun Co. 25 Harrison Avenue, Boston, Massachusetts, 02111 (617) 426-0954

New Jersey
Chinese Kitchen P.O. Box 218, Stirling, New Jersey, 07980 (201) 665-2234

New York
Eastern Trading Co. 2801 Broadway, New York, New York, 10025

The Oriental Country Store 12 Mott Street, New York, New York, 10013

Ohio
Crestview Market 200 Crestview Road, Columbus, Ohio, 43202 (614) 267-2723

Texas
Minika's Oriental Food Mart 2505 West Holcombe Avenue, Houston, Texas, 77003, (713) 668-9850

Washington D.C.
Da Hus Market Company 623 H Street, NW, Washington, D.C. 20005, (202) 371-8888

Indian food and equipment

Arizona
G&L Import-Export Corp. 4828 East 22nd Street, Tuscon, Arizona, 85706, (602) 790-9016

Manila Oriental Foodmart 3557 West Dunlap Avenue, Phoenix, Arizona, 85021, (602) 841-2977

California
Indian Food Mill 650 San Bruno Avenue East, San Bruno, California, 94014, (415) 583-6559

Connecticut
India Spice & Gift Shop 3295 Fairfield Avenue, Fairfield, Connecticut, 06605, (203) 384-0666

Florida
Grocery Mahat & Asian Spices 1026 South Military Trail, West Palm Beach, Florida, 33436, (407) 433-3936

Illinois
Indian Groceries & Spices 7300 St Louis Avenue, Skokie, Illinois 60076, (708) 674-2480

Maryland
India Supermarket 8107 Fenton Street, Silver Springs, Maryland, 20910, (301) 589-8423

Massachusetts
India Groceries Oak Square, Boston, Massachusetts, 02111, (617) 254-5540

New Jersey
Maharaja Indian Foods 130 Speedwell Avenue, Morristown, New Jersey, 07960, (210) 829-0048

New York
Indian Groceries and Spices 61 Wythe Avenue, Brooklyn, New York, 11211, (718) 963-0477

Ohio
Crestview Market 200 Crestview Road, Columbus, Ohio, 43202 (614) 267-2723

Pennsylvania
Gourmail Inc. Drawer 516, Berwyn, Pennsylvania, 19312 (215) 296-4620

Texas
MGM Indian Foods 9200 Lamar Boulevard, Austin, Texas, 78513, (512) 835-6937

Southeast Asian food and equipment

Arizona
Kempo Oriental Market 5595 East 5th Street, Tuscon, Arizona, 85711, (602) 750-9009

Massachusetts
Yoshinoya 36 Prospect Street, Cambridge, Massachusetts, 02139, (617) 491-8221

Minnesota
M.F. Oriental Food 747 Franklin Avenue, Minneapolis, Minnesota, 55404, (612) 870-4002

New York
Katagiri Company 224 East 59th Street, New York, New York, 10022, (212) 755-3566

Siam Grocery 2745 Broadway, New York, New York, 10024 (212) 864 3690

Canada

Dah'ls Oriental Food 822 Broadview, Toronto, Ontario, M4K 2P7, (416) 463-8109

Hong Kong Emporium 364 Young Street, Toronto, Ontario, M5B 1S5, (416) 977-3386

U-Can-Buy Oriental Food 5692 Victoria Avenue, Montreal, Quebec, H3W 2P8

New Zealand

Chinese Food Centre Davis Trading Company Ltd, Te Puni Street, Petone, 568-2009

South Africa

Akhalwaya and Sons Gillies Street, Burgersdorp, Johannesburg, (11) 838-1008

Kashmiris Spice Centre 95 Church Street, Mayfair, Johannesburg, (11) 839-3883

Haribak and Sons Ltd 31 Pine Street, Durban (31) 32-662

United Kingdom
Chinese food and equipment

Chung Wah 31–32 Great George Square, Liverpool L1 5D2 (051) 709-2637

Janson Hong St Martins House, 17–18 Bull Ring, Birmingham B5 5DD, (021) 643-4681

See Woo Supermarket 18–20 Lisle Street, London WC2, (071) 734-9940

Wing Lee Hong 8 Edward Street, Leeds LS2 7NN (0532) 457203

Wing Yip 395 Edgware Road, Cricklewood, London NW2 6LN (081) 450-0422

Indian food and equipment
M. and S. Patel 372–382 Romford Road, London E7 8BS (081) 472-6201

Rafi's Spice Box c/o 31 Schoolfield, Glemsford, Suffolk, CO10 7RE (mail order)

The Spice Shop 115–117 Drummond Street, London NW1 2HL (071) 387-4526

South-east Asian food and equipment

Duc Cung 122 Upper Clapton Road, London E5, (081) 806-0241

Golden Gate Hong Kong Ltd 14 Lisle Street, London WC2 (071) 439-8325

Loon Fung Supermarket 42–44 Gerrard Street, London W1, (071) 437-7332

Matahari 102 Westbourne Grove, London W2, (071) 221-7468

Ninjin 244 Great Portland Street, London W1, (071) 388-2511

Sri Thai 56 Shepherds Bush Road, London W6, (071) 602-5760

Australia

Korean, Japanese and Oriental Food Store 14 Oxford Street, Sydney 2000

Oriental Import 406a Brighton Road, Brighton, South Australia

INDEX